For Bob,

MW00810181

FEWER W
·······································
MORE IMPACT
·······································
GREATER INFLUENCE

SHARPENING YOUR POINT

Winning the **Battle** for Communication Efficiency

Leesa Wallace & Kathy McAfee

Foreword by Jim Horan
Author of *The One Page Business Plan*

With gratitude,
Leesa Wallace

 INDIE BOOKS
INTERNATIONAL

ISBN-10: 1-947480-72-3
ISBN-13: 978-1-947480-72-8
Library of Congress Control Number: 2019913116

The Sharpening Your Point Process™, The PARE Strategy™, The Building Blocks Methodology™, and The Handling a Challenge Strategy™ are pending trademarks of Leesa Wallace.

Designed by Joni McPherson, mcphersongraphics.com

INDIE BOOKS INTERNATIONAL, INC.
2424 VISTA WAY, SUITE 316
OCEANSIDE, CA 92054

www.indiebooksintl.com

Dedication

To our many wonderful clients who understand the importance of communication and see its connection to leadership effectiveness. We applaud your willingness to invest in your people and their potential.

Contents

Foreword

You're frustrated! You are a great listener and even better in your written and verbal communications, but something is wrong!

Too many of your ideas, projects, programs and initiatives are not being fully supported, approved or implemented on time, within budget and achieving the results you promised.

Could it be you are misunderstood too frequently?

Many people believe the greatest risk to their future is their competitors. I believe the far greater risk is not being understood. Not being understood by your manager, direct reports, peers, suppliers, vendors, investors, Board... to say nothing about your clients, customers and employees. If you are misunderstood, you can't achieve your vision or goals.

Leesa Wallace and Kathy McAfee understand why we are frequently misunderstood. We talk too much, we don't say the right things, and we spend too much time storytelling. The authors are right, we don't know how to be clear and effective in our communications.

Sharpening Your Point is a simple, practical, very powerful handbook for highly efficient communications. Whether you are an established leader or an early-career professional, the next level of success requires you learn how to talk differently! Leesa and Kathy give you the tools to cut the fluff, filler and b*llsh*t from your presentations and discussions.

Sharpening Your Point will introduce you to a new way of communicating at work. The authors give you the tools, processes and real-life examples to help you be brief, be brilliant and successful in all of your communications.

You will win more business, achieve more results and be more effective by Sharpening Your Point!

Jim Horan

Best-selling author, speaker, consultant and President of The One Page Business Plan Company

Part 1

Stop

Chapter 1

Are You A Wild Bore?

We knew a Wild Bore. His name was Frank. Let us tell you about him.

We were sitting in a large conference room with fifteen of our colleagues within the talent management function. Our boss, Frank (name changed to protect the innocent), was going to be briefing us on results from a senior management survey. These weren't just any results. These results were feedback from the direct reports of the senior leadership team. This had never been done before in the organization. Ever. It was a big deal. And our team would be seeing the information first.

The senior leadership team was, predictably, anxious to get this information, and so were we. It was our job as the talent management team to understand both the results and the implications of the results. This was essential so the senior leadership could understand what it all meant and what they needed to do with the information. If we didn't "get it," we knew the senior leadership team wouldn't either—they would reject the results, rationalize, or justify. That outcome would be both a disappointing setback for our team and a lost opportunity for our organization as a whole.

Our team gathered for a preview of the information two weeks before the big day. After thanking us for being there, Frank showed his first PowerPoint slide, titled *Agenda*, and read it out loud to us. And, there on the screen was our one-hour agenda laid out in bullet points. Thirteen bullet points, to be exact. They were:

- Results for Competency 1
- Results for Competency 2
- Results for Competency 3
- Results for Competency 4
- Results for Competency 5
- Results for Competency 6
- Results for Competency 7
- Results for Competency 8
- Aggregate Results for Competencies 1–8
- Senior Leader Narrative Data
- Comments and Narrative for Competencies 1–4
- Comments and Narrative for Competencies 5–8
- Areas of Strength and Weakness

Frank showed his second slide: Results for Competency 1. He showed graphs, charts, numbers, and visuals we couldn't read. He started talking about normative data and mean averages. He talked about Likert scales and cross-rater inconsistency. And we all wanted to put hot sticks into our eyes.

You've experienced this, right? Someone is sharing information, giving an update, leading a discussion, and you have no idea where they are going. You're saying to yourself, "And your point is…?" No structure. It is communication gone wild. And you're tuning out. You're bored. We were in the grip of the Wild Bore.

Wild Bores do real damage. They damage their own reputation by not being able to "bottom line" their communication. They focus on the *trivial many* and not the *vital few*. And, worst of all, they waste everyone's time, including yours. But wait, there's more.

Wild Bore Proliferation

If left unchecked, Wild Bores continue to breed more Wild Bores. Pretty soon your organization is filled with them. Not good. Here's an example of how it happens.

Remember Frank? We accused him of being a Wild Bore. And while that was a weakness, Frank did have some real strengths—including the ability to spot and hire great talent. One such superstar was Louise. She was two years out of college and already had acquired an impressive list of skills and experiences. We welcomed Louise into our talent management team and looked forward to her many contributions.

And then we noticed it. During meetings and discussions, Louise struggled to communicate her thoughts and ideas in a coherent fashion. Most of the time, she remained silent. But other times, when we could see she was mustering up the courage, she would just start rambling in way that felt more weekend-conversational than business-appropriate. We couldn't figure out where she was going or what point she was trying to make. We felt for her, but we also felt for us. When Louise was in the room, our meetings and discussions were becoming longer and more painful.

We sensed that Louise knew she had a problem. And it became apparent that our boss, Frank, knew it as well. As her manager, Frank had tried to coach Louise on multiple occasions. He recognized that she was intelligent, creative, and had a great deal of talent and potential. That's why he had hired her. She was early in her career and was still getting accustomed to the demands of the workplace and the company culture. Frank did what he could to model best practices in communication; he felt what he had done in the past had worked quite well for him and his career. If only Louise would follow his lead. Turns out, she did.

Now Louise and Frank have their own monsters to deal with. In fact, each and every one of us bears the same risk—a sudden takeover by a long-winded, data-dumping, unconscientious, rambling communicator who resides inside of us. For the purposes of this book, we will refer to this monster as the Wild Bore.

No, we are not misspelling it. We, the authors of this book, do not mean a wild boar, the animal (genus and species *Sus scrofa*), although, there are some ironic parallels between the animal—wild boar—and this inner monster—Wild Bore. Dig this (no pun intended):

- According to the Huntercourse.com blog, experienced hunters say that wild boar can be even more dangerous to hunt than a bear. Equipped with thick, razor-sharp tusks, and a razor-sharp mind (hogs are the fourth most intelligent animal in the world) a wild boar can weigh a staggering 660 pounds and exhibit unpredictable behavior. The blog site offers this survival tip: "Pick your tree ahead of time so you can climb out of harm's way if ever you're being chased."[1]

- Human intervention has caused the spread of distribution further, making the wild boar species one of the widest-

---

[1] Brent McNamee, "The World's Most Dangerous Game to Hunt," Huntercourse.com, November 9, 2011, https://www.huntercourse.com/blog/2011/11/the-worlds-most-dangerous-game-to-hunt/.

ranging mammals in the world. Its wide range, high numbers, and adaptability have led the wild boar to become an invasive species.

Invasive species? Unpredictable behavior? Razor-sharp mind? Survival tip—get out of harm's way? Why then, yes, wild boars and Wild Bores are equally dangerous creatures, especially in the workplace. Let us explain further.

When you let your Wild Bore lead the discussion, you are at risk of the following negative results and disappointing outcomes:

- Unproductive meetings
- Delayed decisions
- Confusion and frustration
- Lost opportunities
- Damaged credibility
- Employee disengagement
- Fewer prospective clients
- Stalled careers

"When Wild Bores lead the discussion, you are at risk of negative results and disappointing outcomes."

Preserve And Protect

It turns out that communication is a lot harder than it seems. Whether you are an established leader or an early-career professional who has desires and ambitions to be recognized as an emerging leader, communication will play a pivotal role in your career growth and organizational success.

And that's why we are writing this book for you. We want to introduce you to a different way of communicating at work. We call it the art of *communication efficiency*. By reading this book and applying its proven principles, you will not only eradicate the Wild Bore within, but you will preserve and protect your credibility, your confidence, and your career. Are you ready to dig in?

Chapter 2

Be Brief. Be Brilliant. Be Done.

Frank didn't know any better. He did what he always did and it got him, well, pretty much what he'd always gotten—a reputation as a Wild Bore. Problem was, he didn't know how to help anyone else (like Louise) get better because he relied on what he'd been told to do.

Chances are, Frank was likely taught to communicate with the *just-in-case* method. "*Just in case* someone listening to you has a question about XYZ, you better talk about it before the question is asked." Or, "*Just in case* someone might disagree with you, you better be ready to counter the argument or defend your position." Or, "*Just in case* folks don't understand things in the way in which you are explaining them, you should probably have other ways to explain it." This way is wrong. Period. The point of engaging with other people is to encourage questions, dialogue, dissent, and discussion; not to avoid it, not to avoid them.

> *"The point of engaging with other people is to encourage questions, dialogue, dissent, and discussion; not to avoid it, not to avoid them."*

Do you have a case of *just-in-case*? Lots of folks do. Let's test it out. Check yes or no below if you do this. Be brutally honest. Promise, we're not judging.

☐ Yes ☐ No 1. In situations where I need to get my point across (e.g., meetings, updates, discussions), I think about all the topics and information I need to cover.

☐ Yes ☐ No 2. I start with PowerPoint to begin putting my information together.

☐ Yes ☐ No 3. I get rattled or lose focus if someone asks a question I wasn't prepared for.

☐ Yes ☐ No 4. I get nervous or rattled if someone challenges me when I'm speaking or trying to get a point across.

☐ Yes ☐ No 5. If I project my handouts onto the screen, people can read the information easily.

☐ Yes ☐ No 6. I have a clear sense of the beginning, middle, and end of my discussion.

☐ Yes ☐ No 7. My listeners have a clear idea of what they should do as a result of hearing me speak.

☐ Yes ☐ No 8. People listening to me always know why they should care about the topic.

☐ Yes ☐ No 9. When I speak, my point is always clear to those listening.

☐ Yes ☐ No 10. I give listeners the big ideas or headlines before getting into the details.

☐ Yes ☐ No 11. Within ninety seconds of me speaking, my listeners know why they are there, what I want them to do, and why they should do it.

Scoring:

One point for Yes answers to questions 1, 2, 3, 4: Subtotal ____

One point for No answers to questions 5, 6, 7, 8, 9, 10, 11: Subtotal ____

Add Subtotals for your Total Score: _____

Even a score of *one* may make you a victim of *just-in-case*.

The Problem With Just-In-Case

The *just-in-case* method is not only boring, it's also inefficient. Think about a baseball game in which the batter, after hitting to the outfield, runs to first, then to home, then cuts across the pitcher's mound to get to third, doubles back to second, and then touches third base before running home. It sounds silly, but this is what happens when we use the just-in-case method to communicate.

What do we recommend that you do instead?

Just Enough

Replace your just-in-case practice with a Just-Enough mindset. Think about it: There are three questions—and *only* three questions—everyone listening to you is asking:

1. Why am I here?

2. What do you want me to do?

3. Why should I?

We believe that if you can't articulate the answers to those three things within ninety seconds, you are at high risk of becoming a Wild Bore. And if you can, you are well on your way to communication efficiency.

What exactly do we mean by communication efficiency? It means that a message sender presents information clearly and concisely, without excess verbiage.

"The point of engaging with other people is to encourage questions, dialogue, dissent, and discussion; not to avoid it, not to avoid them."

Who has the responsibility to deliver a clear and concise message? Why, that would be you, the facilitator, whenever you are in charge of leading the discussion.

And what benefits does communication efficiency offer you and your career? Here's why you should embrace the mantra, "Be brief. Be brilliant. Be done."

- It takes less time to get your main points across to others.

- Listeners are more likely to pay attention to you.

- Listeners are more likely to find your message appealing when it is delivered in an efficient manner.

- Reducing unnecessary words minimizes the potential for confusion and misunderstanding of your message.

- Listeners (including the leaders in the room) may recognize your brilliance and potential for advancement.

- Knowing when to stop talking increases the opportunity for you to listen, breathe, and learn from others.

- Having the ability to communicate efficiently will bolster your confidence and prepare you for higher-level discussions.

There are easy ways to increase communication efficiency and we'll walk you step by step through the process in chapters 4-9. But first, let us share some examples of how we, the authors, were once Wild Bores…and wildly inefficient communicators.

Chapter 3

Been There. Done That.

Yes. It's true. At one time in our careers, we were both Wild Bores. In fact, it's a weakness we continue to fight on a daily basis. Perhaps we should start a mutual organization and call it Wild Bores Anonymous (WBA). Our purpose could be "To enable members to stay clear and concise and to help other Wild Bores achieve communication efficiency." Just imagine attending one of these meetings.

Member: "Hi. My name is Kathy, and I'm a Wild Bore."

Group: "Hi, Kathy."

Member: "It's been three months since I bored my colleagues with a long, rambling explanation, detailing everything I knew on the subject at hand, just in case they asked."

OK. We are just joking, but we know what it's like to do the hard work of communicating efficiently. And we have experienced the difficult lessons and high costs of doing it wrong. We'd like to share our personal stories and memories of when each of us lost the battle for communication efficiency.

Kathy's Story

I grew up believing that I would one day be a writer. I simply loved words, and I liked to use a lot of them. In fact, my nickname was Chatty Kathy. Somewhere along the way, I convinced myself that I was paid by the word. The more words I used, the more money I would make. You might laugh at this; even today, I find myself repeating this expression in jest, but deep down, perhaps I still hoped that it might be true.

During my early career as a corporate marketing professional, I had several mentors who tried to convince me that *less was better*. One such mentor was Brian, who begged me to contain my written reports to one page. I found a way to meet his requirements by reducing the font size and narrowing the margins. Even then, my reports often spilled onto to page two and three. I had so much to say.

I remember once when I was interviewing for a job with a company. It wasn't just any company or any person; in fact, it was the president of the LEGO Group in North America. In my job search, LEGO was my number one target company. I literally had dreams of how cool it would be to work there. So, I thought I'd go straight to the top. I pitched an idea in writing and mailed it to the president. And a miracle happened—he granted me an interview. OMG. This was my big moment. As I sat in his office, I felt like I belonged there.

We started with some small talk to ease into the discussion and to get to know each other. Then he asked me the question, "So what are you looking for? Do you want a job? Are you looking to do some consulting? How can I help you?"

I responded, "I don't know. What do you think I should do?"

He looked surprised by my response and was quiet for a few seconds.

The awkward silence was enough to propel me into a thirty-five-minute dissertation. I outlined each scenario—employee, consultant, joint-venture partner—with a level of detail that even surprised me. When I came up for air, I glanced at the wall clock in his office. I couldn't believe that so much time had passed. He stood up and extended his arm to shake my hand. He thanked me for coming in and sharing my ideas. Then he walked me to the doorway and handed me off to his executive assistant.

I knew it was game over. I had bored the man and it had cost me my dream job.

Leesa's Story

I worked for ten years at a Very Big Insurance Company whose name shall not be spoken. This company was known for great products and a *ruthless* focus on cost control. How ruthless? A true story, often repeated: An executive, who shall also remain nameless, was walking by a large garbage bin. He dove into it, retrieved a three-ring binder, held it up and bellowed, "Who threw this binder away? It's perfectly good. Do you want new binders, or do you want a bonus?"

Learning and development initiatives were not funded, and the word "training" was considered a four-letter word. The good news? I was able to do whatever I wanted to develop leaders and emerging talent—as long as it didn't cost anything.

It turns out, not developing leaders was costing the Very Big Insurance Company quite a bit—in turnover, legal claims for wrongful discharge, poor management practices, and industry reputation.

And then the company got a new division president.

I saw my opportunity and had a meeting with the president. I talked about and gave examples of the costs of poor management. I outlined a leadership development curriculum that could mitigate the problems we had and, at the same time, develop the managers and future leaders in the organization.

I had him at hello. Or so I thought.

The president was excited about my initiative and invited me to speak to the entire senior team about it. I walked into the board room, saw the president at one end, smiled and began. I started talking about all the different programs and how long each would take. I was interrupted midsentence by the chief operating officer: "How long did you say this was going to take? A year? Man, if we have leaders who don't know what they're doing, I'd let them go rather than spend a year of time on them."

I can't even remember what my response was, but I know that it wasn't very coherent. I was rattled, but I was determined to get through this and have the team get on board the way in which the president was. I decided to switch tactics and talk about cost. Again, I was cut off midsentence. This time the CFO had something to say. And so did the head of marketing. And the head of the legal department. In fact, I didn't make any of the key points I had prepared so carefully. I looked at the president as he very slowly shook his head.

I had bombed. I wanted to talk about the real costs of *not* doing something about developing leadership talent: turnover, lawsuits, poor morale, missed deadlines. Instead I talked—rambled, really—

about everything *but* those things. If I had known then what I know now, that meeting would have been very different.

Why You Should Trust Us

We have shown you our underbellies. We have admitted to you that we are flawed human beings. These learning experiences have given us the motivation to create a new and different way of communicating, especially in the context of leading discussions at work. Over the past fifteen years, we have spent countless hours developing, field testing, and refining the strategies and principles contained in this book. We have done so with the sole intention of helping other professionals, like you, to have more successful, fulfilling careers. A key part of ensuring that positive outcome will be your ability to have productive discussions with clear and concise communication.

> *"A key part of ensuring a positive outcome will be your ability to have a productive discussion with clear and concise communication."*

We believe that you will also benefit from the advice, perspective, and insights from two authors in one book.

Leesa Wallace is known as The Performance Architect. She eats, sleeps, and breathes performance. In her role as learning strategist and consultant, Leesa works with organizations who want people to lead boldly, listen intently, question curiously, and speak clearly. She disturbs the comfortable and comforts the disturbed. Organizations come to Leesa when they lack leaders who are ready to fill the pipeline and assume greater levels of responsibility. Her Build-a-Better-Leader Method helps organizations identify and address leadership development needs. Leesa guides individuals, teams, and organizations to identify their most critical learning and development needs and then works with them to create solutions that have real impact. (All that, and she's super fun to work with.)

Coauthor Kathy McAfee brings a different set of skills to the table. With her marketing DNA and a blood type *C-positive for creative*, she is passionate about helping people position themselves more effectively. She believes in the power of putting people and ideas together to create new opportunities. In her role as an executive presentation coach and professional speaker, she works with organizations who want to build a stronger pipeline of leaders, and with individuals who want to become outstanding in their chosen fields. She particularly loves to work with business leaders who want to become thought leaders by learning how to be more influential when they speak in public, sell their ideas, and connect with others. (All that, and she's very motivating, which is why she is known as America's Marketing Motivator.)

But It's Not About Us. It's About You

We are here to talk about communication efficiency. Because millions of dollars and thousands of careers are being waylaid by boring discussions and inefficient communication. We believe that when you sharpen your point and use fewer words, you will have more impact and greater influence.

We know this because we have trained thousands of professionals—including engineers, bankers, corporate audit staff, IT consultants, marketing, and sales—who have become more successful in their work using our method.

We want you to start using the strategies in this book to lead better discussions. If you do, you will be more effective, productive, respected, and successful. If you don't, you will continue to be regarded as a Wild Bore.

In this book we will introduce three key abilities you must master to become an efficient communicator:

1. Opening the discussion

2. Organizing your thoughts

3. Handling a challenge

So, now that you know why you need to stop doing what you've been told to do in the past (by people like Frank), let's dive into exactly what you should start doing.

Part 2

Start

Chapter 4

Why Am I Here?

Have you ever taken a lesson or gotten additional coaching on something you already know how to do? For example, improving your golf swing? Or playing the piano more fluidly? Or learning new ways to hit a backhand in tennis? Or learning how to make pasta from scratch? It could be anything. And when you meet with your teachers, instructors, or coaches—if they are good—what is the first thing they ask you? "Show me what you *usually* do," or "What are you already doing?"

They want a baseline from which to work.

We are asking you to do the same. We want to see how you *usually* open up a discussion, conversation, update, or any situation in which you have information to share.

Get A Baseline

Instructions

1. Think about a presentation or professional communication situation—either current or past—and write down what you would say (or what you said) in the first sixty seconds of speaking.

2. Now, time yourself. If you said it in fewer than sixty seconds, add more information until what you say *lasts a full sixty seconds.*

_____

_____

_____

_____

_____

_____

_____

_____

_____

_____

_____

_____

_____

_____

This, dear reader, is your baseline. We will be asking you to revisit it later. For now, just mark this page and get ready to sharpen your point.

Leesa's Baseline

In chapter 3, coauthor Leesa shared a baseline: her epic bomb in front of the senior leadership team. Though she's trying to forget it, she does have a pretty good recollection of what she said to open the discussion. It went something like this:

> Hello, everyone. Thanks so much for having me come today. And thank you, Eric, for making time for this on your agenda. Leadership development is really important, and I want to go over a yearlong curriculum that will help us build better leaders going forward. As you can see on this slide, the program starts with Leading Self and the skills needed for that. Between sessions, participants will read important books on leadership and will have the opportunity to lead discussions on the key ideas with the others in the program. The second part of the curriculum focuses on Leading Others. Participants will practice how to listen more effectively, ask better questions, handle performance issues, set goals, and develop potential...

The Idea In Brief

PARE Strategy is a way to open a discussion, talk, presentation, or meeting in a clear, concise, and compelling way.

Within the first minute of talking, your listeners always, always, *always* want to know three things and only three things:

1. Why am I here?
2. What do you want me to do?
3. Why should I?

The PARE Strategy is a framework that helps you articulate these three things clearly, concisely, and convincingly. And the naming convention, PARE, is intentional. Pare means to diminish or reduce. Paring down your opening helps you to answer these questions with efficiency and to engage your listeners in a more meaningful, collaborative, and influential way.

But first, the big picture. The entire PARE opening strategy follows. We'll show you step by step how you can apply it. The PARE Strategy is composed of eight easy pieces. Here's your first glance at the PARE Strategy.

PARE Strategy

Topic What?	Context Statement Why Now?

Position
I think, believe, feel

Ask
I want you to …

Rationale
If you do …
If you don't …

Example
We know this because…

Key Point # 1	Key Point # 2	Key Point # 3

Check in with Audience

Let's Start At The Very Beginning—A Very Good Place To Start

We are going to go into depth on each component of the PARE Strategy, but we need to begin with topic and context. This is the jumping-off point for communication efficiency and quickly answers the most critical question for listeners: Why am I here? It's important to get this out of your mouth quickly in order to grab listeners' attention and hold it.

As you can see from Leesa's example—painfully retold—her first words missed what she was going to talk about and *why* the audience should even bother listening. Our tendency is to data-dump up front and get into detail way too soon. And because articulating the topic and context statement can be simple, we tend to overcomplicate and over-talk at the beginning.

> *"Our tendency is to data-dump up front and get into detail way too soon."*

So, we need to discuss how to articulate your topic and context quickly, because you have limited time to give information in an influential and concise way. We know that articulating topic and context clearly is the most important part of getting your point across and want you to practice doing this before you learn anything else. If you don't, your audience will be immediately left wondering "Why am I here?" and if they're not clear on that, they will start to tune out. All you have to do is reread Leesa's epic bomb to see how true that is.

Topic: What Are You Talking About?

Quite simply, *Topic* is what you will be talking about—the main topic of the discussion, the central issue, etc. Note how brief and clear these examples are.

Topic Examples

- "Today we're discussing the role of context in communication."
- "We need to talk about communication efficiency."
- "Today I'll be talking about leadership development."
- "At issue today is the lack of female representation at the executive level."

As you can see, there are slightly different ways to state your topic, but these examples all answer clearly and efficiently, "What are you talking about?"

What The Heck Is Context?

Dictionary definitions of *Context* are all similar. Since we love communication efficiency, we define it a bit differently. We define context as simply *why* you are talking about your topic—or *why now*? Context helps you to establish (or reestablish) the importance of the topic for your listeners.

Now it's simply a matter of putting topic and context together. Let us give you a few examples of effective and ineffective ways to articulate topic and context. We'll start by using parts of Leesa's baseline example and share others that we've heard.

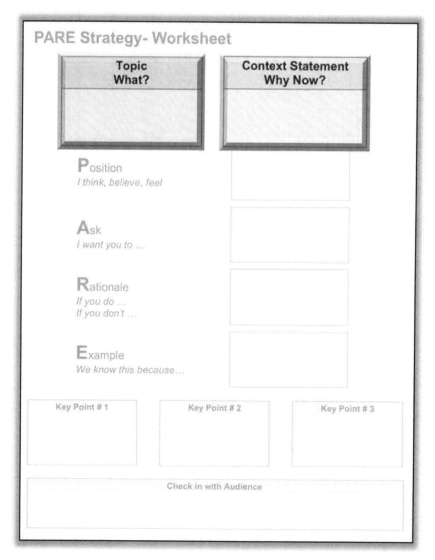

What do you immediately notice about the *before* and *after* statements? Do the after statements let the listener know what is going to be talked about and why now?

Before: "Hello, everyone. Thanks so much for having me come today. And thank you, Eric, for making time for this on your agenda. Leadership development is really important, and I want to go over a yearlong curriculum that will help us build better leaders going forward."

After: "Hello, everyone. Today we'll be talking about leadership development [Topic] because for the past ten years, training has been a four-letter word in this organization [Context]."

Before: "My rotational assignment was a very eye-opening experience for me, and I learned so much that I'd like to share with you today, the most important being how we can better underwrite and maintain our margins."

After: "I will be talking about my rotational assignment [*Topic*] because it's ending soon and there were some key discoveries you need to know about [*Context*]."

Before: "We want to share with you the results of the senior leadership survey and go over each competency area—one through eight—the aggregate data for the competencies, narrative data from the senior team, narrative data for all the competencies, and next steps. We'll then open up for questions."

After: "In the next hour, we'll be going over the results of the senior leadership survey [*Topic*] because the senior team is anxious to see what folks are saying about them and we need to be clear on how we present results [*Context*]."

Before: "We'll be going over the results of your audit, next steps, what might have gotten in the way, and what areas the audit showed were working well. Here's our agenda for our discussion."

After: "Today we'll be going over your audit results [*Topic*] because we are about to end it, and there are some actions you'll need to take before we do [*Context*]."

Six Steps For Putting Topic And Context To Work

1. Use a sentence-starter to begin the discussion.

2. The fewer words the better.

3. Sometimes it works better to state the context before the topic.

4. Be efficient, but don't be abrupt.

5. You can be broad or narrow in identifying the topic.

6. When articulating context, think deeply about your audience. From their perspective, why is it relevant and why now?

A Deeper Dive

Let's examine each one of these six steps to give you a fuller understanding of why they are important and how they will benefit you as the facilitator of the discussion.

1. Use the following sentence-starters until you get comfortable improvising.

    • "Today, we are/I am going to talk about

    _____ [*Topic*]

    because_____ [*Context*]."

- When articulating the context, try to look at the topic from the listener's point of view. Why would you want to introduce or reestablish the importance of the topic?

- "Today, I want to update you on the project. You said the project needed to be done in two weeks, and we have three days left until then."

2. You don't need many words for this. Try to articulate your Topic and Context Statement in thirty-five words or less. Count them and see what you can cut.

3. Once you feel comfortable with articulating your topic and context statement, feel free to drop the sentence-starters or mix up the order.

   - "Our due date for the project is three days out, and we need to talk about where we are on that."

4. Don't confuse communication efficiency with being abrupt. Introduce yourself (if necessary), welcome your listeners, and thank them for being there or listening to you. Create rapport appropriately before you begin your PARE. But *once you start*, stay with the strategy we recommend.

> *"Don't confuse communication efficiency with being abrupt."*

5. Identify your topic in a way that is most compelling for your listeners. That means determining whether you articulate narrowly ("Today we are going to discuss our fourth quarter result") or more broadly ("We need to talk about women in

leadership roles"). Think about what will be most important to your audience and frame it accordingly.

6. Context is hugely important in helping listeners understand the *why* behind *what* you will be talking about. What will be the most impactful *why* for them?

   - Are they concerned about cost? Try this: "We are over budget and we need to get a handle on things."

   - Are they driven by quality? Try this: "This is critical because our efficiency scores are down significantly."

   - Are they driven by being in the loop? Try this: "You said this was the most critical piece of the project and milestones are coming up."

Practice Makes Permanent

Below are some very broad topics. If you had people listening to you, what would you say to articulate the topic and context?

If it makes sense, you could switch the order and articulate your context first and then the topic. "Our lease is almost up *[context]* so we need to talk about our new office location *[topic]*."

Here are sentence-starters to get you going.

Office Dress Code

[*Topic*] "Today we need to talk about office dress code…"

[*Context Statement*] …because _____."

Cost Control

[*Topic*] "We are here to discuss_____…"

[Context Statement] …because _____."

Women in Leadership

[Topic] " _____..."

[Context Statement] …because _____."

Going Green

[Topic] " _____..."

[Context Statement] "…because _____."

What's Next?

So, now that you can tell listeners what you'll be talking about and why they should listen, you need to develop the rest of your opening to the discussion. Flip the page and you'll see the next critical piece of the PARE Strategy—your Position.

Chapter 5

What's Your Position?

H ave you seen *The Far Side* single-panel cartoon by Gary Larson titled *Boneless Chicken Ranch*? Look it up on the internet (keywords: boneless chicken ranch gary larson). You'll see a winding driveway leading to the entrance of a ranch or farm. A custom sign hangs above a large gated entrance. In scripted font, the sign reads, *Boneless Chicken Ranch*. Strewn about the fence and in surrounding areas of grass are chickens. At first, they appear to be sleeping; maybe they are dead? But then you get the joke. *They have no bones.* They are boneless chickens. They can't stand around and cluck as normal chickens do.

Using only these three words, *boneless chicken ranch*, and a very creative illustration, this irreverent cartoonist not only makes us laugh, but also makes us think. Boneless chickens would have a very hard time standing up for themselves. Literally, they would fall over. They have no internal support structure: no skeletal system, no backbone, no bones. This would limit their upward mobility in any organization.

And that's what can happen to you if you fail to take a position when you are leading a discussion. You are more likely to fall over, fall apart, and go nowhere.

That is what the *P* in the strategy PARE stands for: Position. You must take a position in any discussion you lead. Right, wrong, popular, or unpopular, you must state what you think, feel, believe, or know to be true. This is the backbone of the discussion that you wish to lead, the core of the message that you need to send. And while you may end up with a very different agreement at the end of the discussion, without a solid starting point, it's hard to begin.

The Idea In Brief

Position

What do you think feel, believe about the topic? This should be a very short sentence. Begin with "I think," "I believe," or "I feel." This is not the time to support your position; just tell people what it is.

Many professionals we have coached and trained over the years have expressed concern that they were not in position to state a position. They preferred to defer all declarative statements and decisions to the boss or the senior ranking officer in the room. They felt that it was inappropriate and presumptuous to offer a recommendation or opinion unless the leader specifically asked for it. And while this may be the normal protocol in some organizations (e.g., military), in the modern business world, most organizations need and want their people to share ideas, recommendations, and points of view. This is important to drive innovation, competitiveness, and growth. As a style of leadership, *command and control* is out; collaboration and teamwork are in.

> *"You must take a position in any discussion you lead. Right, wrong, popular, or unpopular, you must state what you think, feel, believe, or know to be true."*

Coauthor Kathy shared a personal story in which she failed to clearly and concisely answer the question posed by an executive leader. He asked her during an informational interview, "So what are you looking for? Do you want a job? Are you looking to do some consulting? How can I help you?" She responded, as if without a backbone, "I don't know. What do you think I should do?" Let's rewrite that history and see how differently the conversation might have gone if Kathy had taken a solid position.

Executive: "So, what are you looking for?"

Kathy: "I believe that I would be a great asset to the LEGO organization."

Executive: "How so?"

Kathy: "As a member of your brand team, I can contribute my innovative thinking, consumer marketing experience, and collaborative working style to accelerate the development of the LEGO brand."

Executive: "Can you give me an example?"

Kathy: "Yes, I can." (Conversation continues...)

As you can see, this discussion is headed in a more productive direction. The communication is two-way, and with short, focused statements, it is also more efficient. This is certainly better than the long, boring, mind-numbing, monologue-style communication that happened the first time.

A Very Short Sentence

Remember, you are just starting your discussion and you have sixty seconds to let listeners know why they are there, what you want them to do, and why they should do it. When stating your position, you are declaring what you think, feel, believe, or know to be true. This should be a very short sentence. It is not the time to support your position. It is not the time for diving into details. That comes later in the discussion. Just tell people what your position is. The fewer words you use, the better off you will be. Simplicity and clarity are key to communicating your position.

The Good And The Bad

Let us give you a few examples of effective and ineffective position statements. These examples were taken from a training class with a group of emerging leaders in a rotational program working for a midsized regional bank.

We captured the *before* statements from live video recordings of their baseline practice presentations in preparation for a formal meeting with the senior leadership team. We then rewrote the *after* statements to model the *P* for their positions using the PARE Strategy.

Before: "The most important thing I learned in this rotational assignment was how important accuracy and attention to detail are. Something as small as misinterpreting the difference between a final

PARE Strategy

Topic What?	Context Statement Why Now?

Position
I think, believe, feel

Ask
I want you to …

Rationale
If you do …
If you don't …

Example
We know this because…

Key Point # 1	Key Point # 2	Key Point # 3

Check in with Audience

availability date and a maturity date of a loan could mean disaster when funding a construction loan." (Forty-six words)

After: "I believe that accuracy and attention to detail are critical factors when funding a construction loan." (Sixteen words)

Before: "Lastly, in this rotational, due diligence is extremely important. You need to know your borrowers and you need to know your deals and have a very strong credit background to be able to pick out any mistakes that you might find. A lot of times we get submitted financials, tax returns, and invoices and you need to be able to verify that information and know what you're looking for in order to assess if there is a problem and that's where a strong credit background comes in." (Eighty-seven words)

After: "I believe that a strong credit background is essential for an effective due diligence process." (Fifteen words)

Before: "My number one focus coming into this first rotation was really to develop a credit foundation and skills that I could build on as I progressed throughout my career. I really felt that my experience in middle market really solidified those skills and built the foundation that I wanted to build off of." (Fifty-three words)

After: "I felt that my experience in middle market gave me a solid credit foundation and skills that I can build my career from." (Twenty-two words)

What do you immediately notice about the *before* and *after* statements? What changes have been made? Which do you prefer? Which is more efficient? Which communication—the *before* or the *after*—do you think would be more effective with a group of senior leaders in the room?

Position Statement Examples

In our workshops, we give our participants random cards with *fun* topics—some work-related, other more personal in nature. We then ask them to formulate a PARE opening so they can practice leading a group discussion on that topic with their peers. This exercise challenges them to think about topics that they might not have considered before. It also requires them to think on their feet, deciding what position to take on their assigned topic. We tell them that it doesn't matter what position they choose. We are not here to debate the issue. What we want them to demonstrate is their ability to communicate a position in an efficient and confident manner in front of their peers.

Here are a few **Position** statement examples from those classroom exercises using the *fun* topics (although one could argue that these topics aren't really fun; they are pretty serious in nature).

Office Dress Code. "I feel that a casual dress code would increase productivity and reduce stress at work." (Fifteen words)

Cost Control. "I think we have the opportunity to significantly reduce office expenses." (Eleven words)

Personal Branding. "I believe that consistently managing one's personal brand is essential to career management." (Thirteen words)

Communication. "I believe that communication skills can either make or break an engineer's career." (Thirteen words)

Open Work Space. "I feel that people can be more productive and connected when they work in close proximity to one another." (Nineteen words)

Caffeine. "I think that caffeinated beverages help our employees to increase focus and productivity." (Thirteen words)

Pets At Work. "I feel that allowing pets at work will have a very positive impact on employee morale and well-being." (Eighteen words)

Going Green. "I believe that it is our responsibility to reduce waste in a more intention way." (Fifteen words)

Women in Leadership. "I believe that the financial performance of our organization will improve with more women in leadership roles, starting today." (Nineteen words)

Six Steps For An Effective Positioning Statement

1. Keep it a short, simple, declarative statement. The fewer words the better.

2. Begin the positioning statement with one of these sentence-starters: I think, I believe, I feel.

3. Reduce any nonessential words. Use the word count feature on your computer to calculate exactly how many words you've used in your positioning statement.

4. Avoid compound sentences that include multiple ideas with independent clauses joined by a comma, semicolon, or conjunction.

5. Avoid upspeak—that annoying habit of turning every statement into a question by raising the pitch of your voice at the end of the sentence. The upspeak vocal pattern will take the wind out of the sails of your positioning statement.

6. Commit your positioning statement to memory. Don't allow yourself to *wing it*. Practice. Practice. Practice.

Practice Makes Permanent

Your turn: Read the topic below and draft your own position statement on these sample topics. Feel free to be creative in your answers. These are strictly for practice of the technique.

Social Media. What do you think, feel, or believe about this topic?

_____

_____ (____ words)

Online Dating. What do you think, feel, or believe about this topic?

_____

_____ (____ words)

Chocolate. What do you think, feel, or believe about this topic?

_____

_____ (____ words)

Medical Marijuana. What do you think, feel, or believe about this topic?

_____

_____ (____ words)

Autonomous, Self-driving Cars. What do you think, feel, or believe about this topic?

_____

_____ (____ words)

International Travel. What do you think, feel, or believe about this topic?

_____

_____ (____ words)

Disneyland. What do you think, feel, or believe about this topic?

_____

_____ (____ words)

The more you practice the skill of stating a position clearly and concisely, the better you will become at it, and the more confident you will feel, look, and sound. By investing your time and energy in learning to state your position on a variety of topics, you will be building your thought-leadership muscles. Of course, listening to others' views and positions is just as important. That's part of what makes a productive discussion and collaborative workplace.

> _"By investing your time and energy in learning to state your position on a variety of topics, you will be building your thought-leadership muscles."_

When you become a student of communication efficiency, the world is your classroom. Any situations at work or in life can become an opportunity for you to practice stating your position using the PARE Strategy. Simply take the topic at hand, observe how experts are communicating their position, and rewrite it using what you've learned in this chapter. Yes, you can build a better position statement. With practice, it will become second nature to you. Do this when:

- You read an article in the news

- You listen to the radio or a talk show

- You observe how others state their position during meetings

- You read about trends in your industry

- You watch TED Talks

- Other places and spaces _____

"Listening to others' views and positions is just as important. That's part of what makes a productive discussion and collaborative workplace."

What's Next?

Now that you've gotten the hang of stating your position in a clear and concise manner, what do you do next? What do your listeners need and want to know from you next? Dive into the next chapter, where you will learn more about the A in the PARE Strategy.

Chapter 6

What Do You Want Me To Do?

I magine that you are sitting in a meeting room, listening to one of your colleagues present a plan for a new enterprise resource planning system (ERP). You know that this will be a major disruption for the organization, but in the long run, it is what's needed to gain and sustain business excellence and market leadership. At least, that's what you've heard from the powers that be. During the meeting, your colleague outlines the entire implementation plan, from start to finish. Your head is starting to ache. And a single question keeps circling around in your mind: "What am I supposed to do about this?"

It's all so nebulous and overwhelming.

After about forty-five minutes of talking at you, the speaker says something that brings you back to full consciousness. "This is going to be a massive undertaking. I could really use your full support on this." Now you are really confused. What exactly are you expected to do? What does he mean by "full support"? In some ways, you think, this could be easy. You could just nod your head politely and say, "You got it." Then you can walk out of the meeting room without really making any commitments. You think to yourself, "Sure, you have my support, but you are not going to get any of my resources. I'm short-staffed and fully tapped out as it is."

And there you have it: the instant when momentum comes to a grinding halt. Without a clear and specific "ask," the probability of any action following such a discussion is near zero. The meeting has effectively turned into a do-nothing. You and your colleagues have been let *off the hook* when the meeting leader did not make a clear request for action. Chances are, you will have to repeat this meeting discussion several more times in order to make progress toward the goal. What a big waste of time—yours and theirs.

Ask And You Shall Receive

OK, maybe you won't get everything you ask for every time. But without asking for what you want and need, you won't get it. People can't read your mind. Some individuals are more intuitive and can sense what you are inferring without you having to say it. But the majority of people are direct listeners. If you don't spell it out directly and clearly, they don't hear it.

That is what the *A* in the PARE Strategy stands for. *A* is for **Ask**. To be an efficient communicator, you need to discipline yourself to make a clear, specific request for action. You must answer the second of the three critical questions that every listener needs to know from you:

1. Why am I here?
2. What do you want me to do?
3. **Why should I?**

The Idea In Brief

Ask

What specific action do you want your listener to take? Caution: Get out of the "support" trap. Do not ask "for your support." What does "support" actually look like? Get specific.

Get Comfortable With The Uncomfortable

Many professionals we have coached and trained over the years have found it awkward and uncomfortable to ask for something during a discussion, meeting, or presentation. They have told us that they don't want to sound too "salesy" or to be pushy or presumptuous. They prefer to just report the facts and let others ascertain what needs to be done about it. But there's power in the ask. If you can muster the courage and confidence and match that with the communication efficiency you are learning in this book, people will start listening more intently to what you have to say. You might also find that they start implementing your recommendations more often. Lastly, they may start to see you as an emerging leader with potential to take on more responsibilities. Who could ask for more?

PARE Strategy

Topic What?	Context Statement Why Now?

Position
I think, believe, feel

Ask
I want you to ...

Rationale
If you do ...
If you don't ...

Example
We know this because...

Key Point # 1	Key Point # 2	Key Point # 3

Check in with Audience

What Are You Really Asking Us to Do?

If you've ever been to a political rally or heard a politician speak at a conference, town hall, or televised debate, you've probably witnessed the best and the worst of communication. Polished, experienced, and influential, when these speakers take the floor, they are there to get a reaction. Few moderators have the courage to give the hook to long-winded government officials for fear of appearing rude or receiving potential retribution. Meanwhile, the audience suffers as these Wild Bores drone on and on and on from the podium.

One recent example comes to mind from one of our coauthors. While attending an annual meeting of a large chamber of commerce, the state governor was invited to give a few remarks. The conference planners told the governor that he had eight minutes to speak. Secretly, the conference team planned for ten minutes, knowing the governor's reputation for going long. He spoke without any notes and was clearly enjoying himself. At minute twenty-two, the meeting planners and the audience were becoming visibly annoyed. And that's when the governor made his ask. He said, "I'm calling on your help." And those in the audience who were still awake were thinking, "What the heck does that mean? What kind of help are you asking for? What exactly do you want me to do? I'm already bleeding here listening to you bore me to death."

So, what could the Governor have done to be a more efficient communicator, other than prepare written remarks and practice ahead of time to ensure he could deliver his message in under eight minutes? We suggest that the governor could have made a clearer and more specific ask. For example:

Before: "I'm calling on your help."

After: "I need you to call your state representative in the next forty-eight hours and tell them to vote Yes on Senate Bill 123. And ask your friends to do the same."

Now, which do you think (before or after) stands a greater chance of being implemented?

Ask Examples

Let's take a look at a few other *before* and *after* examples of asks that would be more effective. We will use a variety of situations, both professional and personal, to help make our point. Read each set of examples out loud. Which feel more powerful to you? How might you change the wording of the *after* examples to make them even more efficient and effective?

Before: "It would be really nice if someone else would help out around the house now and then."

After: "I'm asking you to take out the trash every Wednesday morning and to bring in the empty trash can from the curb in the afternoons, starting tomorrow."

Before: "It would be so helpful if some of you might consider donating to our cause."

After: "I'm asking you to become a sustaining donor, contributing $50 or more each month to our charity, through a recurring credit card payment."

Before: "We really need more people to help out on this project to meet our deadlines."

After: "Please sign this requisition for a new full-time employee so that we can meet the aggressive deadlines on this important project."

Before: "I would really love to work for your company, and I think I have a lot to contribute."

After: "I want you to hire me as your next IT leader."

Before: "Everyone says what a great couple we make, and, you know, we love each other. So, I was thinking that maybe we should, well, you know, get married?"

After: "Will you marry me?"

Before: "If we could get an infusion of capital, with the right partner, we could hire more people and invest in more equipment which would allow us to expand into international markets. That would be so awesome."

After: "We are asking for your investment of $5 million into the business this year."

> *"There's power in the ask. If you can muster the courage and confidence and match that with communication efficiency, people will start listening more intently to what you have to say."*

Make It A Bold Ask

Les Brown, an American motivational speaker, author, and former television host, is quoted as saying, "Shoot for the moon. If you miss, you will still be standing among the stars." Let's apply his philosophy to our topic at hand.

When preparing your PARE Strategy to open the discussion, we encourage you to explore the possibility of making a bolder ask. Why ask for ten cents when you could ask for ten dollars? Why ask for one hundred dollars when you could ask for one thousand dollars? You never know the capacity that people have to give. You won't know what's possible until you test it out. If your request is rejected, you will most likely survive. If your bold ask gets agreed to, well then, your reward is not only a greater impact on your organization, but a greater surge of personal confidence.

Six Steps For An Effective Ask

1. Don't use *squishy* language that is vague or subject to misinterpretation: things like, "I am asking you to all get on board with the project," or "I'm asking for your commitment to the project." (And, yes, "support" is squishy language.)

2. Be very specific. Ask for something that you can measure afterwards.

3. Focus your ask on one or two critical things. If you ask for too many things, you dilute the power and probability of any action being taken.

4. Be bold. Stretch the ask and see what's possible.

5. Look them in the eye when you make your ask.

6. State your ask as just that: a statement, not a question.

Practice Makes Permanent

The ask is a natural next step once you have stated the topic, context, and your position. Let's build upon the examples that we laid out in chapter 5.

Office Dress Code

[*Topic and Context Statement*] "Today we're discussing office dress code because the employees have asked to revisit the policy."

[*Position*] "We believe that a casual dress code would increase productivity and reduce stress at work."

[*Ask*] "We'd like you to authorize a new policy allowing jeans on Fridays."

Cost Control

[*Topic and Context Statement*] "Our budgets are due within a month, and we're all here to talk about expense control." (Note: in this example the Context is first, followed by the Topic.)

[*Position*] "I think we can reduce office expenses by cutting back on the number of printers on each floor."

[*Ask*] "We'd like to present this idea at your next senior executive meeting."

Personal Branding

[*Topic and Context Statement*] "We are graduating soon, so we need to discuss how we show up to others—our personal brand. (Note: in this example the context is first, followed by the topic)

[*Position*] "I believe that consistently managing one's personal brand is essential to career management."

[*Ask*] "I'd like us to all update our LinkedIn profile summaries and write them in the first-person voice within the next three business days."

Communication

[*Topic and Context Statement*] "We're here to talk about communication because we got direct feedback that it needs improvement."

[*Position*] "I believe that communication skills can either make or break an engineer's career."

[*Ask*] "I need you to distill the technical data into meaningful messages that the executives can understand and use to make decisions at the next meeting."

Women in Leadership

[*Topic and Context Statement*] "We need to discuss women in leadership because this is something that hasn't yet been addressed formally."

[*Position*] "I believe that the financial performance of our organization will improve with more women in leadership roles, starting today."

[*Ask*] "We ask you to allocate $150,000 for a new women's leadership accelerator cohort program to create a pipeline of strong female leaders."

Open Work Space

[*Topic and Context Statement*] "Open concept living is all the rage, and it's coming to the work environment. We need to talk about this."

[*Position*] "I believe that people can be more productive and connected when they work in close proximity to one another."

[*Ask*] "I'm asking you to identify which areas could be converted to an open work space and submit recommendations within one week."

Caffeine

[*Topic and Context Statement*] "Let's talk caffeine because, let's face it, we depend on it."

[*Position*] "I believe that caffeinated beverages help our employees to increase focus and productivity."

[*Ask*] "We need you to authorize this requisition for new Keurig coffee machines to be placed in every break room."

Pets at Work

[*Topic and Context Statement*] "We are here to discuss reducing stress in the workplace. This was identified as the number two issue in our recent employee survey."

[*Position*] "I feel that allowing pets at work will have a very positive impact on employee well-being and stress reduction."

[*Ask*] Write it below:

_____

_____

Going Green

[**Topic and Context Statement**] "We are launching our new sustainability program and we need to talk about going green."

[**Position**] "I believe that it is our responsibility to reduce waste by changing our packaging and educating our customers."

[**Ask**] Write it below:

_____

_____

What's Next?

So far in the discussion, you have told your listeners why they are here and what you want them to do. You now need to answer the unspoken question that everyone is thinking: *Why should I?* Your ability to provide a convincing rationale could make or break the outcome of your discussion. By diving into the next chapter, you will dramatically increase the probability of a successful outcome. If you skip it, well…you're toast.

Chapter 7

Why Should I?

I f you've ever been around young children, you've probably heard
this after asking them to do something. And your ask is likely very
clear:

You: "Darling, it's time to clean your room."

Child: "Why?"

You: "Because your room is a mess, and school starts tomorrow."

If the sweet one is slightly more daring, it might sound like this:

You: "Sweetie, I'm asking you to clean your room. Please."

Child: "Why should I?"

You: "Because I said so."

Or, if the child is acting like a true stubborn brat:

You: "Precious, I'm going to say this one last time: clean your room."

Child: "You can't make me!"

You: "Oh, yes I can."

Now let's apply this to the work world. We know when you ask your colleagues or clients to do something, you are not dealing with children who don't want to do what you are asking.

Or are you?

The difference, we believe, is that the adults who listen to you may not *say* these things out loud. But, believe us, they are thinking it. And they have every right to.

Randy Hall, CEO of 4th Gear Consulting, sums it up well in his blog:

> *"Consider every conversation we have, meeting we lead, and interaction in which we are involved. Those events will either have a positive impact, a negative impact, or no impact on the others involved. Every exposure to us ends in one of those three possibilities. How we choose to have our conversations largely determines which one of those outcomes happen. How many times do we deliver a message or have a conversation that, while focused clearly on what we wanted others to do differently, actually has no impact, or even a negative impact on what they actually do?"*[2]

We believe articulating the rationale for why your listeners should do what you're asking is critical to the forward movement of the discussion. That's what the *R* in the PARE Strategy stands for. It helps you have a more positive, influential impact. It answers these questions that your listeners are quietly thinking about: (1) "If I do

---

[2] Randy Hall, "Why People Don't Do What You Say," 4th Gear Consulting, March 26, 2012, http://www.4thgearconsulting.com/blog/why-people-dont-do-what-you-say/.

what you're asking, what's in it for me?" or (2) "What might happen if I don't do what you're asking?"

The *R* in the PARE Strategy takes care of the last of the three critical questions every listener needs to hear:

- Why am I here?

- What do you want me to do?

- **Why should I?**

The Idea In Brief

Rationale

A statement that provides a compelling reward to the listener for doing what you ask, or a clear consequence for not doing it.

Why Linkage Matters

How can you ensure that your Ask and your Rationale are compatible and strongly linked? Think of them as magnets that are incredibly difficult to pull apart. It might sound something like this:

> *"I need you to call on your state representative within the next forty-eight hours to vote yes on Senate Bill 123 [Ask] because if you don't, this measure will be defeated and the music program in our schools will be eliminated [Rationale]."*

See how tightly linked the Ask and the Rationale are?

Here's an example of an *unlinked* Ask and Rationale.

> *"I need you to call on your state representative within the next forty-eight hours to vote yes on Senate Bill 123. I'm asking because this is really important for our children."*

And *voila*! The speaker has just transformed back into a Wild Bore as he watches his audience completely tune out, eyes rolling into the backs of their heads.

While the statement "This is really important for our children" is a significant idea, it lacks the power of consequence or benefit that drives much of human behavior. We would also argue that this type of rationale is a bit obvious, and there is nothing compelling about stating the obvious. If you want to engage your listeners and really motivate them to action, you have to dig deeper for a compelling rationale. Otherwise, you haven't answered the third critical question that every listener absolutely *must* have answered: "Why should I do what you're asking?"

"If you want to engage your listeners and really motivate them to action, you have to dig deeper for a compelling rationale."

What Will Happen If You Do Or You Don't Do?

Ray Jimenez, PhD, is the chief architect at Vignettes Learning, an e-learning and technology services company. In a video, Dr. Jimenez provides insight into the importance of providing your audience with strong rationale—the consequences and benefits of taking action or not. And while the context for his video is about setting learning objectives for e-learning programs, this excerpt from his video also applies to Sharpening Your Point situations:

"I would recommend that if you are writing content or making a presentation or doing a webinar, go back to where the consequences are and the benefits if they do or they don't do the content. In fact, in all of my presentations I always start with the concept 'What will happen if you do or you don't do.' Because that is what grabs people's attention and that's what matters to people and the impact on their lives."[3]

Rationale Examples

Let's keep building on what we've done in chapter 6 and demonstrate how to make the ask and rationale clear, compelling, and compatible. Here are some *before* and *after* examples of how to do so.

Taking Out the Trash Can

Before:

[*Ask*] "I'm asking you to set out the trash after 8:00 a.m. on Wednesday..."

[*Incompatible/Weak Rationale*] "...because that would be a good idea given that we live in the woods."

---

[3] Vignettes Learning, "Story-Based ELearning Idea: Learning Objectives That Truly Matter at Work," YouTube, April 16, 2019, https://www.youtube.com/watch?v=7KfzEUm8xc8.

PARE Strategy

Topic What?	Context Statement Why Now?

Position
I think, believe, feel

Ask
I want you to ...

Rationale
If you do ...
If you don't ...

Example
We know this because...

Key Point # 1	Key Point # 2	Key Point # 3

Check in with Audience

After:

[*Ask*] "I'm asking you to set out the trash after 8:00 a.m. on Wednesday..."

[*Compatible/Strong Rationale*] "...because if you don't, the bears will get into it at night and it will be all over the place in the morning and you'll have to clean it up."

Charitable Donation

Before:

[*Ask*] "I'm asking you to become a sustaining donor, contributing $50 or more each month to our charity..."

[*Incompatible/Weak Rationale*] "...because giving makes us feel good."

After:

[*Ask*] I'm asking you to become a sustaining donor, contributing $50 or more each month to our charity."

[*Compatible/Strong Rationale*] "If you do, you will be part of curing childhood diabetes forever."

Hiring More Employees

Before:

[*Ask*] "Please sign this requisition for a new full-time employee..."

[*Incompatible/Weak Rationale*] "...because we are really short-staffed for the project."

After:

[*Ask*] "Please sign this requisition for a new full-time employee."

[*Compatible/Strong Rationale*] "If you don't, we won't have enough staff to meet our deadlines or our contractual commitments to the client."

Marriage Proposal
Before:

[*Ask*] "Will you marry me?"

[*Incompatible/Weak Rationale*] "It's been long enough and I'm tired of waiting."

After:

[*Ask*] "Will you marry me?"

[*Compatible/Strong Rationale*] "If you do, you'll never have to wonder if I'm the one who got away."

Business Investment
Before:

[*Ask*] "We're asking for your investment of $5 million dollars into the business this year..."

[*Incompatible/Weak Rationale*] "…because we haven't invested in our business properly."

After:

[*Ask*] "We're asking for your investment of $5 million dollars into the business this year."

[*Compatible/Strong Rationale*] "If you don't, we are ripe for a venture capital group to buy us out."

 Five Steps For An Effective Rationale

1. Be compatible. Your Rationale must be strongly linked with your ask. Use the sentence-starters, "If you do…" or "If you don't…" when articulating the Rationale. It almost forces you to connect to the Ask.

2. Be brief. This is not the time for a long explanation.

3. Be clear. Vague inferences, generalizations, and the obvious are like white noise to your listeners.

4. Be compelling. Understand what drives your listeners. How will they be personally affected by the outcome? Find a motivation (positive or negative) that really matters to them.

5. Beware. There will be time later to defend or expand on your Rationale. For now, you simply want to grab and hold attention in a compelling and efficient way.

Practice Makes Permanent

The Rationale is a natural next step once you have stated the topic, context, position, and ask. Let's build upon the examples that we laid out in chapter 6.

Office Dress Code

[*Topic and Context Statement*] "Today we're discussing office dress code because the employees have asked to revisit the policy."

[*Position*] "We believe that a casual dress code would increase productivity and reduce stress at work."

[*Ask*] "We'd like you to authorize a new policy allowing jeans on Fridays..."

[*Rationale*] "...because if you do, people will be far more productive than they are now."

Cost Control

[*Topic and Context Statement*] "Our budgets are due within a month, and we're all here to talk about expense control." (Note: In this example the context is first, followed by the topic.)

[*Position*] "I think we can reduce office expenses by cutting back on the number of printers on each floor."

[*Ask*] "We'd like you to present this idea at your next senior executive meeting."

[*Rationale*] "If you don't, the senior team will lose an opportunity to make a relatively painless budget cut."

Personal Branding

[*Topic and Context Statement*] "We are graduating soon, so we need to discuss how we show up to others—our personal brand. (Note: In this example the context is first, followed by the topic.)

[*Position*] "I believe that consistently managing one's personal brand is essential to career management."

[*Ask*] "I'd like you all to update your LinkedIn profile summaries and write them in the first person within the next three business days."

[*Rationale*] "If you do, you will increase your chances of being hired within two months of graduating."

Communication

[*Topic and Context Statement*] "We're here to talk about communication because we got direct feedback that it needs improvement."

[*Position*] "I believe that communication skills can either make or break an engineer's career."

[*Ask*] "I need you to distill the technical data into meaningful messages that the executives can understand and use to make decisions at the next meeting."

[*Rationale*] "If you don't, executives will continue to relay bad or incorrect information about our project."

Women in Leadership

[*Topic and Context Statement*] "We need to discuss women in leadership because this is something that hasn't yet been addressed formally."

[*Position*] "I believe that the performance of our organization will improve with more women in leadership roles, starting today."

[*Ask*] "We ask you to budget $150,000 for a new women's leadership accelerator cohort program to create a pipeline of strong female leaders."

[*Rationale*] "If you don't, we may lose key talent to our direct competitors, who already have these programs in place."

Open Work Space

[*Topic and Context Statement*] "Open concept living is all the rage, and it's coming to the work environment. We need to talk about this."

[*Position*] "I believe that people can be more productive and connected when they work in close proximity to one another."

[*Ask*] "I'm asking you to identify which areas could be converted to an open work space and submit recommendations within one week."

[*Rationale*] "If you don't, we may miss out on attracting the younger generation to our organization."

Caffeine

[*Topic and Context Statement*] "Let's talk caffeine because, let's face it, we depend on it."

[*Position*] "I believe that caffeinated beverages help our employees to increase focus and productivity."

[*Ask*] "We need you to authorize this requisition for new Keurig coffee machines to be placed in every break room."

[*Rationale*] Write it below using the following sentence-starters:

"Because if you do…

_____

_____."
"

"Because if you don't…

_____

_____."
"

Pets at Work

[*Topic and Context Statement*] "We are here to discuss reducing stress in the workplace. This was identified as the number-two issue in our recent employee survey."

[*Position*] "I feel that allowing pets at work will have a very positive impact on employee well-being and stress reduction."

[*Ask*] Write it below:

_____

_____."
"

[*Rationale*] Write it below using the following sentence-starters:

"Because if you do...

_____

_____ "
.

"Because if you don't...

_____

_____ "
.

Going Green

[*Topic and Context Statement*] "We are launching our new sustainability program and we need to talk about going green."

[*Position*] "I believe that it is our responsibility to reduce waste by changing our packaging and educating our customers."

[*Ask*] Write it below:

_____

_____ "
.

[*Rationale*] Write it below using the following sentence-starters:

"Because if you do...

_____

_____ "
.

"Because if you don't...

_____

_____ "
.

What's Next?

So far in the discussion, you have told your listeners why they are here, what you want them to do, and why they should do it. You now need to provide a brief example or support. What makes you so sure your position, ask, and rationale are correct? Your ability to provide support will help further enhance your credibility and influence. In the next chapter, we'll show how to do just that.

Chapter 8

Do You Have Proof?

If you are going to assert a Rationale, you had better be able to back it up. Wild Bores will tell you all about why you should do something, but give no support or examples to support their claims. Said differently, this is your opportunity to separate fact from fiction.

First, let's get on the same page with objective definitions of facts and opinions. We appreciate this set from the Key Differences website:

> "A fact is something that has actually taken place or known to have happened which can be validated with pieces of evidence. A fact can be an event or information, based on real occurrences. A fact is nothing but a verifiable truth or reality which are agreed upon by a consensus of people....The term 'opinion' is defined as the personal view or judgment about a subject, that may or may not be substantiated by the facts or positive knowledge. It is what a person thinks or feels about something or someone. Opinion is highly influenced by a person's feelings, thoughts, perspective, desires, attitude, experiences, understanding, beliefs, values, etc., which cannot be tested by concrete evidence."[4]

---

[4] "Difference Between Fact and Opinion (with Comparison Chart)," Key Differences, October 28, 2017, https://keydifferences.com/difference-between-fact-and-opinion.html.

Below is a chart that helps to sum up the comparison of facts and opinion.[5]

Facts	Opinions
Refer to something that can be verified or proved to be true	Refer to a judgement or belief about something
Are based on objective reality	Are based on subjective statement
Are not debatable	Are debatable
Are possible to verify	Are not possible to verify
Have the power to influence others	Have the power to influence others

We know what you're probably thinking: "Wait! Didn't you just tell us that our listeners want to know what we think, believe, or feel? That stating our position (the *P* in the PARE Strategy) was a strong way to open?"

We did, and it is. We want you to tap into your listeners emotion *and* their logic center, and we want you to do it intentionally. It's time to back up your *P*osition, *A*sk, or *R*ationale with an example. That's the last piece, the *E* in the PARE Strategy.

The Idea In Brief

Example

A short piece of evidence, data point, statistic, or anecdote that provides support for your Position, Ask, and/or Rationale.

---

[5] Ibid., chart modified

PARE Strategy

Topic What?	Context Statement Why Now?

Position
I think, believe, feel

Ask
I want you to …

Rationale
If you do …
If you don't …

Example
We know this because…

Key Point # 1	Key Point # 2	Key Point # 3

Check in with Audience

A PARE Is A PEAR By Any Other Name

So far, we have suggested a particular order for opening your discussion. But sometimes, it's more natural and appropriate to have the example come before the ask. Your strategy then goes from a PARE (*Position, Ask, Rationale, Example*) to a PEAR (*Position, Example, Ask, Rationale*). You have a choice in structuring the order and flow.

PARE/PEAR Examples

Let's build on what was laid out in chapter 7. You'll notice that we are alternating between PARE and PEAR formats to demonstrate the flexibility in the strategy. Also, please note the statements shown below in the [*Example*] sections are not necessarily factual. They are for illustrative purposes only.

Office Dress Code (PARE)

[*Topic and Context Statement*] "Today we're discussing office dress code because the employees have asked to revisit the policy."

[*Position*] "We believe that a casual dress code would increase productivity and reduce stress at work."

[*Ask*] "We'd like you to authorize a new policy allowing jeans on Fridays..."

[*Rationale*] "...because if you do, people will be far more productive than they are now."

[*Example*] "The Harvard School of Medicine just did an extensive, ten-year study that showed productivity increased by 25 percent when employees were allowed to wear jeans to work."

Cost Control (PEAR)

[*Topic and Context Statement*] "Our budgets are due within a month, and we need to talk about expense control."

[*Position*] "I think we can reduce office expenses by cutting back on the number of printers on each floor."

[*Example*] "Printer use has been reduced by 50 percent since we implemented our 'Go Green' strategy reducing the amount of attachments to emails."

[*Ask*] "We'd like you to present this idea at your next senior executive meeting."

[*Rationale*] "If we don't, the senior team will lose an opportunity to make a relatively painless budget cut."

Personal Branding (PARE)

[*Topic and Context Statement*] "We are graduating soon, so we need to discuss how we show up to others—our personal brand. (Note: In this example the context is first, followed by the topic.)

[*Position*] "I believe that consistently managing one's personal brand is essential to career management."

[*Ask*] "I'd like you all to update your LinkedIn profile summaries and write them in the first person within the next three business days."

[*Rationale*] "If you do, you will increase your chances of being hired within two months of graduating."

[*Example*] "Indeed.com claims that they are twice as likely to reach out to potential candidates when their summaries are written this way."

Communication (PARE)

[*Topic and Context Statement*] "We're here to talk about communication because we got direct feedback that it needs improvement."

[*Position*] "I believe that communication skills can either make or break an engineer's career."

[*Ask*] "I need you to distill the technical data into meaningful messages that the executives can understand and make decisions with at the next meeting."

[*Rationale*] "If you don't, executives will continue to relay bad or incorrect information about our project."

[*Example*] "As you know, all of the project milestones were missed because the executives got more than 100 emails a day."

Women in Leadership (PEAR)

[*Topic and Context Statement*] "We need to discuss women in leadership because this is something that hasn't yet been addressed formally."

[*Position*] "I believe that the performance of our organization will improve with more women in leadership roles, starting today."

[*Example*] The Gallup organization study showed that Fortune 100 companies with at least 25 percent female leadership at the top level outperformed competitors by double-digit margins."

[*Ask*] "We're asking you to budget $150,000 for a new women's leadership accelerator cohort program to create a pipeline of strong female leaders."

[*Rationale*] "If you don't, we may lose key talent to our direct competitors who already have these programs in place."

Open Work Space (PEAR)

[*Topic and Context Statement*] "Open concept living is all the rage, and it's coming to the work environment. We need to talk about this."

[*Position*] "I believe that people can be more productive and connected when they work in close proximity to one another."

[*Example*] "Inc.com's most recent study showed that millennials' number-one driver was people over profit, and that included a collaborative work space."

[*Ask*] "I'm asking you to identify which areas could be converted to an open work space and submit recommendations within one week."

[*Rationale*] "If you don't, we may miss out on attracting the younger generation to our organization."

Five Steps for An Effective Example

1. Be aware of the difference between your rationale and an example: these are two very different things. Remember, the rationale is *always* connected to the ask. It answers the question, "Why should I?" The example isn't necessarily connected to the ask. It proactively answers what listeners are thinking when you speak. "And you know this because...?"

2. Be honest. Don't make stuff up. Be ready to cite your sources and defend the validity of the information. Your listeners may challenge that. (More to come on handling challenges in chapter 11).

3. Be brief, be brilliant, and be done. If you like data, numbers, and all things quantifiable, you could easily start data-dumping. Keep your Wild Bore in check and pick only one example that best supports your position, ask, or rationale.

4. Be compelling. Understand what drives your listeners. What piece of evidence, data, anecdote, or story will be the most motivating?

5. Be consistent. Use the sentence-starter, "We/I know this because..." There will be opportunities in the future to delete the sentence-starters. For now, use them until the strategy becomes second nature.

Practice Makes Permanent

While articulating an example doesn't answer the three questions directly…

- Why am I here?

- What do you want me to do?

- Why should I?

…it does lend importance and credibility to the answers of those three questions in a logical and influential way. It's the natural next step that links the position, ask, and rationale components together beautifully. Powerfully.

Your turn. Give it a whirl.

Caffeine (PARE)

[*Topic and Context Statement*] "Let's talk caffeine, because, let's face it, we depend on it."

[*Position*] "I believe that caffeinated beverages help our employees to increase focus and productivity."

[*Ask*] "We need you to authorize this requisition for new Keurig coffee machines to be placed in every break room."

[*Rationale*] "Because if you don't, our workers will go out of the office to get their caffeine fix."

[*Example*] Write it below using the following sentence-starter:

We know this because…

_____

_____

Pets at Work (PEAR)

[*Topic and Context Statement*] "We are here to discuss reducing stress in the workplace. This was identified as the number-two issue in our recent employee survey."

[*Position*] "I feel that allowing pets at work will have a very positive impact on employee well-being and stress reduction."

[*Example*] Write it below using the following sentence-starter:

We know this because…

_____

_____

[*Ask*] "I'd like to ask you to convert the empty auditorium into a doggie daycare."

[*Rationale*] Write it below using the following sentence-starters:

Because if you do…

_____

_____

Going Green (PARE)

[*Topic and Context Statement*] "We are launching our new sustainability program and we need to talk about going green."

[*Position*] "I believe that it is our responsibility to reduce waste by changing our packaging and educating our customers."

[*Ask*] Write it below:

_____

_____

[*Rationale*] Write it below:

Because if you don't…

_____

_____

[*Example*] Write it below:

We know this because…

_____

_____

What's Next?

You are almost ready to dig into the details, but not quite yet. First, you have to preview your headlines and check in with your listeners to be sure they are prepared and ready to listen. It's the quickest part of your opening, but critical to communication efficiency.

Chapter 9

Are We There Yet?

How many times have you heard kids say: "Are we there yet?" It's the most annoying question ever, but it's actually fundamental. Your audience is thinking exactly the same thing. Your audience needs to know where you're going to take them, and they might want to have a say in that as well. The last two pieces of the PARE Strategy get everyone moving in the same direction.

> *"If you don't know where you're going, any road will do."*
> **—Mark Twain**

Remember coauthor Leesa's baseline opening from chapter 3? She would like to forget it, too, but we need to revisit it (much to Leesa's chagrin) to illustrate what's missing and why her discussion went off the rails. Here it is:

> *Hello everyone. Thanks so much for having me come today. And thank you, Eric, for making time for this on your agenda. Leadership development is really important, and I want to go over a year-long curriculum that will help us build better leaders going forward. As you can see on this slide, the program starts with Leading Self and the skills needed for that. Between*

sessions, participants will read important books on leadership and will have the opportunity to lead discussions on the key ideas with the others in the program. The second part of the curriculum focuses on Leading Others, and participants will practice how to listen more effectively, ask better questions, handle performance issues, set goals, and develop potential...

First, does it pass the three-question test?

- Why am I here?

- What do you want me to do?

- Why should I?

Clearly not. But it's missing something else critical for listener engagement and understanding: previewing, or bottom-lining, what's to come. We call these key points, and they help direct everything else that follows. As Mark Twain said, "If you don't know where you're going, any road will do."

Figuring out what your key points are and previewing them for the listener will get everyone moving in the same direction, toward the same destination.

The Idea In Brief

Key Points

A way to "bottom line" and preview for your listeners what you'll be communicating more about and what they should be listening for.

It's Not Difficult, Promise

We aren't sure why, but developing key points seems to confuse our participants. To make this easier, think of newspaper or online articles. They all have headlines. And the best, most captivating headlines are usually no more than six to eight words. Since we are all about communication efficiency, we believe you can develop key points with less than that.

A key point is something that you will *eventually* be discussing or speaking about in more depth, and your audience needs to know in your opening to be listening for it. You don't need another page in your PowerPoint deck articulating the agenda for the discussion. Frank, the Wild Bore from chapter 1, had his agenda on slide one of his PowerPoint. Remember it? (Yeah, we don't either.) To refresh your memory, here it is:

Agenda for:

- Results for Competency 1
- Results for Competency 2
- Results for Competency 3
- Results for Competency 4
- Results for Competency 5
- Results for Competency 6
- Results for Competency 7
- Results for Competency 8
- Aggregate Results for Competencies 1-8
- Senior Leader Narrative Data
- Comments and Narrative for Competencies 1-4

- Comments and Narrative for Competencies 5-8
- Areas of Strength and Weakness

Frank failed to headline where he was going by not articulating **Key Points**. Here's what his three key points could have/should have been....and he didn't need a slide for them:

1. Competency Results
2. Narrative Comments
3. Strengths and Weaknesses

"A key point is something that you will eventually be discussing or speaking about in more depth, and your audiences needs to know in your opening to be listening for it."

Ideas For Key Points

Your key points are the headlines of the areas in which you will go into depth to support your position, ask, rationale, or example. These are not all the possibilities, but here are some examples of key points that we frequently see used.

Current Situation	Choices	Implementation Strategy
Communication Plan	Constraints	Challenges
Results	Impact	Next Steps
Possible Solutions	Recommendations	Background
Past Performance	Causes	Case Studies

Once you've decided what your key points are, you simply tell them to your listeners. It might sound something like this: *"So, based on this, we are going to go over three things: competency results, narrative comments, and strengths and weaknesses."*

Key Points Examples

Let's take two of the sample topics we've used in previous chapters and see what they may sound like through introducing the key points. Notice the power of communication efficiency.

Communication

[Topic and Context]	We're here to talk about communication because we got direct feedback that it needs improvement.
[Position]	I believe that communication skills can either make or break an engineer's career.
[Ask]	I need you to distill the technical data into meaningful messages that the executives can understand and use to better make decisions at their team meetings.
[Rationale]	If you do this, you will increase the probability of your project getting approved.
[Example]	For example, last week Chris used the PARE Strategy to lead a very productive discussion with senior leaders. As a result, they approved his project to move to the next phase of development.
[Key Points]	In our meeting today, we will focus on three things: Opening remarks, key messages, and supportive data.

PARE Strategy

Topic What?	Context Statement Why Now?

Position
I think, believe, feel

Ask
I want you to …

Rationale
If you do …
If you don't …

Example
We know this because…

Key Point # 1	Key Point # 2	Key Point # 3

Check in with Audience

Women in Leadership

[Topic and Context]	We need to discuss women in leadership because this is something that hasn't yet been addressed formally.
[Position]	I believe that the financial performance of our organization will improve with more women in leadership roles, starting today.
[Ask]	We ask you to invest in a new women's leadership accelerator cohort program, budgeting $150,000 each year for three years.
[Rationale]	If you approve this, you will strengthen our leadership pipeline and reduce turnover costs for our organization.
[Example]	For example, Catalyst research organization just recently released the list of women CEOs of the top S&P 500. Our main competitor made the list; we did not.
[Key Points]	Today we will examine three things related to our female workforce: P&L impact, the proposed program, and next steps.

Seven Steps For Effective Key Points

1. Focus. Usually two to three key points are enough for any discussion. More makes things worse, not better.

2. Align. Select key points that will support either your position, ask, or rationale.

3. Headlines only. No more than one to three words to headline each of your key points.

4. Use buckets. Choose more general terms and concepts, rather than specifics, as your key points. The specific stuff comes during the middle of the discussion, not the beginning.

5. Exercise patience. Resist the urge go into detail on any of your key points until you finish your PARE opening.

6. Aim for simplicity. Make your key points simple enough that people can remember them in their heads and/or write them down. Avoid complex words or long phrases as your key points.

7. Pause and look. When you are saying your key points, pause briefly between each one and look at a different person. This will help to slow you down and make your key points more memorable and impactful for your listeners.

Practice Makes Permanent

Let's try headlining key points for some of the examples we saw in other chapters. Use the key point examples or create your own to build on the following PARE openings.

Open Work Space

[Topic and Context]	Open concept living is all the rage, and it's coming to the work environment. We need to talk about this.
[Position]	I believe that people can be more productive and connected when they work in close proximity to one another.
[Example]	Inc.com's most recent study showed that millennials' number one driver was people over profit, and that included a collaborative work space.
[Ask]	I'm asking you to identify which areas could be converted to an open work space and submit recommendations within one week.
[Rationale]	If you don't, we may miss out on attracting the younger generation to our organization.
[Key Points]	So, based on this, we're going to talk about three things: 1. _____ 2. _____ 3. _____

Caffeine

[Topic and Context]	Let's talk caffeine, because, face it, we depend on it.
[Position]	I believe that caffeinated beverages help our employees increase focus and productivity.
[Ask]	We need you to authorize this requisition for new Keurig coffee machines to be placed in every break room…
[Rationale]	…because if you don't, our workers will go out of the office to get their caffeine fix.
[Example]	Based on time sheets submitted last week, each employee in our department spent an additional fifty minutes every day to pick up coffee at the local Starbucks.
[Key Points]	So, we need to discuss the following three things to make this happen: 1. _____ 2. _____ 3. _____

Congratulations: You are in the home stretch. You are nearly through your opening. Hang in there; you only need to do one more thing to complete your opening remarks. Are you ready?

Checking In

Imagine an older teenager, almost eighteen years of age. This individual is on the verge of adulthood and is eager to gain true independence. But they are still reliant on the parent/guardian for providing the essentials (i.e., food, clothing, shelter, health care insurance, oh, and let's not forget the subscription to Netflix). This young person is feeling like they can call their own shots, but they know they need to periodically check in with the folks. Because if they don't, all hell will break loose.

In many ways, checking in holds true in a business discussion. The communicator may feel like they are in complete control since they are the one leading the discussion and have the "talking stick," but without the listener's buy in, the discussion may go nowhere. It could just be talk—talk—talk with no real outcomes: no meaningful dialog, no agreement, no sale, no action, no progress.

How do you know if your listener is still with you? At what point do you sense that they might be disengaging? You might be able to read their body language and look for clues (e.g., crossed arms, facial expressions, slumped posture, looking away, yawning, distracted by their digital devices, lack of eye contact, etc.). But then again, you might misread the nonverbal signals they are sending.

> *"Without the listener's buy in, the*
> *discussion may go nowhere."*

The Idea In Brief

The Check-In

A short statement or rhetorical question that serves to validate understanding and engage your listener in the discussion.

Benefits Of Checking In

Behold the power of checking in. With a simple phrase delivered at the right moment, you can reengage your listener. Here are just a few of the benefits of the Check-In: the last part of your PARE Strategy opening.

- Tells you if your audience is following your logic or not

- Grants you implicit permission to move forward

- Gives your audience a feeling of shared power and choice

- Communicates that you are paying attention and that you care about the listener

- Acts as a transition to the next section in the discussion

Cora's *Aha* Moment

Cora is one of those clients you never forget. Her passion for her work is clearly evident in everything she does and how she does it. She is a curious and attentive professional, always ready to learn something new. Perhaps she honed these attributes early in her career while teaching math and science to eighth-graders in middle school. When we met Cora, she was managing leadership development programs for the engineering division of large company in the aerospace and defense industry. Cora hired us to introduce the PARE Strategy to an international audience—a team of technical professionals who were preparing for an important briefing meeting with an American executive vice president who would be visiting their country in a few weeks.

The training session was challenging in several ways: the virtual live-stream technology of the classroom, the multi-lingual aspect, and the cultural nuances that naturally impact communication and understanding. Cora got very excited when we got to the final step of the PARE Strategy—checking in. She felt that checking in would be very useful in helping her international audience feel more engaged, especially given the language barrier. She later explained to us, "Because I'm a fast talker, I often get caught up in the message I am delivering and lose awareness of my audience. When I was teaching in middle school, we were constantly reminded of the importance of evaluating our classroom. Why am I not applying that principle when I'm presenting to adults? The PARE Strategy not only allows me to frame the discussion, it also allows me to be of greater service to my audience."

How To Check In

- Does this make sense?

- Sound like a plan?

- Shall we begin?

- Let's start with... [*state one of your key points*]

- Which area would you like to discuss first?

- Let's move to our first key point.

- If you are ready, let's dive into the first key point.

- Are you with me so far?

- Are you onboard?

- Good to go?

Check-In Examples

Let's keep working with the two sample topics we've used in this chapter and see them through from start to finish using the PARE Strategy. If you were facilitating a discussion on either of these topics, you might choose to use different words or examples. Regardless, pay attention to the flow and efficiency that the PARE Strategy brings to the table. PARE ensures that the three critical questions your audience needs to know (Why am I here? What do you want me to do? Why should I?) are answered in the first ninety seconds of the discussion.

PARE Strategy

Topic What?	Context Statement Why Now?

Position
I think, believe, feel

Ask
I want you to …

Rationale
If you do …
If you don't …

Example
We know this because…

Key Point # 1	Key Point # 2	Key Point # 3

Check in with Audience

Communication

[Topic and Context]	We're here to talk about communication because we got direct feedback that it needs improvement.
[Position]	I believe that communication skills can either make or break an engineer's career.
[Ask]	I need you to distill the technical data into meaningful messages that the executives can understand and use to better make decisions at their team meetings.
[Rationale]	If you do this, you will increase the probability of your project getting approved.
[Example]	For example, last week Chris used the PARE Strategy to lead a very productive discussion with senior leaders. As a result, they approved his project to move to the next phase of development.
[Key Points]	In our meeting today, we will focus on three things: Opening remarks, key messages, and supportive data.
[Check-In]	Are you on board?

Women in Leadership

[Topic and Context]	We need to discuss women in leadership because this is something that hasn't yet been addressed formally.
[Position]	We believe that the financial performance of our organization will improve with more women in leadership roles, starting today.
[Ask]	We ask you to invest in a new women's leadership accelerator cohort program, budgeting $150,000 each year for the next three years.
[Rationale]	If you approve this you will strengthen the diversity of our leadership pipeline and reduce turnover costs for our organization.
[Example]	Catalyst Research recently released its 2019 report and revealed that women currently hold only twenty-four (or 4.8 percent) of the CEO positions at the S&P 500 companies.
[Key points]	Today we will examine three things related to our female workforce: P&L impact, the proposed program, and next steps.
[Check-In]	Let's take a look at the numbers first...

Both of these PARE examples contain less than 125 words each. Is it possible to have more impact and greater influence with fewer words? You bet.

Six Steps For An Effective Check-In

1. Keep it short and simple. The more words you use, the more confusion you sow.

2. No scanning the room. Look at one person (any person) in the eye when you check in.

3. The question "Are there any questions so far?" makes a terrible Check-In during your PARE opening. It's way too early in the discussion. Save that question for later in the discussion.

4. Be careful not to overdo the check-in, or to repeat the same check-in too frequently, as it can become annoying.

5. An effective check-in will elicit a response from the listener (either verbal, nonverbal, or a sound, such as "Uh-huh"), indicating consent that you may continue.

6. Pause for two seconds after you check in. Breathe and then move on.

Practice Makes Permanent

Now it's your turn. Come up with a checking-in phrase that flows naturally for these PARE (or PEAR) Strategy examples. Just fill in the blanks:

Personal Branding—PARE

[Topic and Context]	We are graduating soon so we need to discuss how we show up to others—our personal brand.
[Position]	I believe that consistently managing one's personal brand is essential to career management.
[Ask]	I'd like you all to update your LinkedIn profile summary and write it in the first-person within the next three business days.
[Rationale]	If you do, you will increase your chances of being hired within two months of graduating.
[Example]	Indeed.com claimed that they were twice as likely to reach out to potential candidates when their LinkedIn summaries were written this way.
[Key Points]	So, based on this, we're going to walk you through three things related to your LinkedIn Profile: 1. Your Picture 2. The Headline 3. Personal Summary
[Check-In]	_____ .

Marriage Proposal—PARE

[Topic and Context]	Today we are celebrating our third anniversary since our first date. I'd like to talk with you about the future of our relationship.
[Position]	I think we are ready to the take the next step in our journey together.
[Ask]	I'm asking for your hand in marriage.
[Rationale]	If you say yes, you will enjoy a lifetime of love, laughter and financial security.
[Example]	I know this to be true because my first wife felt the same way. Just kidding...
[Key Points]	If you're game, let's discuss three important decisions: 1. The date 2. The budget 3. And most importantly, the honeymoon.
[Check-In]	_____ .

Office Dress Code—PARE

[Topic and Context]	Today we're discussing office dress code because the employees have asked to revisit the policy.
[Position]	We believe that a casual dress code would increase productivity and reduce stress at work.
[Ask]	We'd like you to authorize a new policy allowing jeans on Fridays...
[Rationale]	...because if you do, people will be far more productive than they are now.
[Example]	The Harvard School of Medicine released an extensive, ten-year study that showed productivity increased by 25 percent when employees were allowed to wear jeans to work.
[Key Points]	So, let's discuss the following three things to make this happen at our workplace: 1. _____ 2. _____ 3. _____
[Check-In]	_____ .

Cost Control—PEAR

[Topic and Context]	Our budgets are due within a month, and we need to talk about expense control.
[Position]	I think we can reduce office expenses by cutting back on the number of printers on each floor.
[Example]	Printer use has been reduced by 50 percent since we implemented our "Go Green" strategy of reducing the amount of attachments to emails.
[Ask]	We'd like you to present this idea at your next senior executive meeting.
[Rationale]	If you don't, the senior team will lose an opportunity to make a relatively painless budget cut.
[Key Points]	So, we need to discuss the following three things: 1. _____ 2. _____ 3. _____
[Check-In]	_____ .

What's Next?

Now that you've practiced and know how to use the PARE Strategy to effectively open the discussion in ninety seconds or less, it's time to figure out what happens next. In chapter 10, you will be introduced to a methodology to better organize your thoughts and determine what content to include in the discussion and what to leave out. These are the building blocks you'll need to facilitate more productive discussions.

Part 3

Start

Chapter 10

What's the Plan?

There is so much you could say to make your point. How in the world will you decide what to include and what to exclude from the discussion? The data is endless, and you never know what your listener might ask or need to know before they can make a decision. Best to bring it all to table. Right? *Wrong.*

You need a way of organizing your thoughts, ideas, and content that will help you have a productive conversation with your listeners. Not too little, not too much, but just the right amount of supportive data to do the trick. But how do you decide? You need a plan and a method to help you make important decisions about the organization and flow of your content.

Introducing the Building Blocks Methodology: a simple, effective, and (if we may be so bold) brilliant way of planning and organizing the content for your discussion. Before you even think of opening presentation software like PowerPoint, map out your game plan using the Building Blocks Methodology. It will save you a huge amount of time and reduce the risk of data proliferation. And you will avoid the anxiety of a near-miss incident, which can happen when you go into the Wild Bore mode of oversharing.

The Idea In Brief

Building Blocks Methodology

Create a simple and logical framework including subpoints to support your position or ask which provides your listeners with just enough information to follow the discussion and to come to agreement.

Benefits of the Building Blocks Methodology

There are many different ways to organize your presentation. Just search Amazon.com under books for "presentation persuasion" or "effective communication skills" and you'll find hundreds of offerings. You might have also attended past courses or trainings at work or in college that introduced methods of organizing your content. We believe that the Building Blocks Methodology is one of the easiest, simplest, most straightforward organizational tools on the market. Here are just a few of the ways in which our method will help you to prepare for a successful discussion:

- Quickly organize your thoughts and content

- Prioritize information in order of importance

- See when you have too much information

- Think spatially, helping you to navigate around the data to make better decisions

- Enhance the order and flow of ideas

- Mitigate risk of data-dumping and proliferation

- Save time on unnecessary slide creation

- Reduce procrastination by helping you to identify core content early in the planning stages

How Much Data And Detail Should You Include In The Discussion?

Up until now, we have encouraged you to stay pretty high-level with the information and ideas you share with your PARE Strategy. But now that you are in the middle of the discussion, it's time to go a bit deeper. You need to make decisions about the specific content, information, and detail that should be introduced as **Sub-Points** under each of your Key Point areas. You may be tempted to show and tell them everything that is available, but that would be a big mistake. For one thing, you don't have enough time to cover all that detail. Plus, that would make for a very boring, overwhelming, and torturous experience for your listener.

The trick to the Building Blocks Methodology is deciding what needs to be included and what to leave out. Here are a few things to consider when choosing your Sub-Points:

- What details are essential, relevant and needed to be shared to ensure a productive discussion?

- What information does the listener need to know in order to be well-informed and make a good decision?

- What details should or could be left out of the discussion because they are nonessential, inconsequential, unrelated, or potentially confusing?

- What information can you put in your "back pocket," to be used if and when you are asked a specific question by a listener?

Transitional Statements Can Help with the Flow

After sharing all of the Sub-Points under each Key Point topic area, consider using a verbal transitional statement to guide the discussion to the next Key Point. This will signal your listeners that you are moving on to a new topic area. Transitional statements have a similar use and effect as the Check-In part of the PARE Strategy.

Your transitional statement might sound something like this:

- Now that we've covered _____ [key point], let's take a look at our second key point, _____.

- Are you comfortable moving on to our second key point, _____?

- Are we all in agreement with _____ [key point 1]?

- Any questions about _____ [key point 1] before we move on to discussing the second key point?

- And that leads us nicely to our second key point topic, _____.

Not A PowerPoint Slide

Do not confuse or use the Building Blocks Methodology with a presentation slide or handout. It was not designed to be public-facing. Its sole purpose is to help you, the facilitator, prepare to lead a productive discussion. Consider the Building Blocks Methodology as a presenter worksheet *only*. If you need visuals or an agenda for your discussion, create something audience-specific.

How Will You Close The Discussion?

You never want to end the discussion with the question, "Are there any questions?"

Why? Because the time to ask and answer questions is in the middle of the discussion, not at the end.

You want to close the discussion in a more professional, confident, and efficient manner. And we have a method to help you do that. We call it the WWW closing. (Just think of the Worldwide Web and how that has changed everything.)

The WWW closing can help you change the impact of your discussion by boosting accountability and action. What does WWW stand for in this case? *Who* does *What* by *When?*

- **Who**: Who is on point to take the next step? Name a person or team of people.

- **What**: Exactly what will they work on? What deliverable have they signed up for (or been volun-told)?

- **When**: What is the timing for their deliverable? List a specific due date or target date for that next step to be accomplished.

The Building Blocks Methodology

OPENING (Use the PARE Strategy)

Provide Relevant Details For Each Key Point

Key Point 1	Key Point 2	Key Point 3

Sub-Point 1	Sub-Point 1	Sub-Point 1

Sub-Point 2	Sub-Point 2	Sub-Point 2

Sub-Point 3	Sub-Point 3	Sub-Point 3

CLOSING (Try the WWW closing – *Who does What by When*)

WWW Closing Examples

Here are three examples of how of how the WWW closing works. Remember the closing is the last thing you do in the discussion. You should get some sign of agreement from your listeners—such as a head nod, a grunt, or some sort of verbal approval (like a *Hallelujah*). Once closed, the discussion is over and folks can move on. It's a beautiful moment in any discussion.

- "In closing, Mary and her team will prepare a list of recommended vendors and circulate it for our comment the week of April 17."
  - *Who*? Mary and her team
  - *What*? Prepare and circulate list of recommended vendors
  - *When*? Week of April 17

- "To summarize our agreements today, Josh will share his engineering materials testing results with us by next Friday. We will meet again in two weeks to determine our team's recommendation to senior management."
  - *Who*? Josh
  - *What*? Engineering materials testing results
  - *When*? Next Friday, and in two weeks

- "Great discussion today. We have agreed to move forward with the Leadership Academy. Next steps: the HR team will work with the procurement team to contract with Leesa Wallace's company on or before November 30 so that we can launch the new program on January 2."

- *Who*: The HR team and the Procurement team

- *What*: Contract with Leesa Wallace's company for new Leadership Academy

- *When*: Finish contracting by November 30, launch program on January 2

Seven Steps For Success With The Building Blocks Methodology

1. Keep it simple

2. Provide just enough information to support your position or your ask

3. No more than three subpoints for each key point category

4. Decide what subpoints to leave out (you can store them in your back pocket)

5. Offer variety in the subpoints to make it engaging for your listener (e.g., case study, illustration, financial analysis, story, demonstration, specific example, interactive exercise, industry report highlights, short video clip, photos, etc.)

6. Use a Transitional Statement before moving to the next key point; something like, "Now that we've discussed *X*, it's time to explore *Y*."

7. Prepare a closing statement. Never end with the question, "Are there any questions?"

Putting it All Together

We are pleased to be able to share with you three real-life client examples of using PARE and the Building Blocks Methodology to prepare for and facilitate important discussions at work. Some of the content in these examples has been changed to protect the privacy of the client.

Example: Building Buy-In for Investments at a Key Supplier

Background: Bill is a technical fellow with an expertise in manufacturing engineering. He works with a leading global aerospace company. In his role, he is a mentor and a coach to peers and younger engineers and advises management on matters of technology assimilation through collaboration. In this particular situation, Bill was helping Tony, one of his engineering colleagues, to prepare for an important meeting with senior management on a critical project. Bill shared with us that Tony, like most engineers, was "reluctant to take a position." But Bill believes you must take a position and you "always have an ask." He finds the PARE Strategy and other tools in this book are "appropriate for tactical conversations and meetings."

[*Topic and Context*] "We are here to talk about the actions necessary to sustain and support performance improvements at a key supplier. Why? Because inaction will impact the largest program on our books today, jeopardizing future deliveries to a program highly valued and closely watched by customers."

[*Position*] "We believe that we have to invest resources now to realize product deliveries and resulting revenue."

[*Ask*] "While we need a total of $2 million over the next two years to complete all activities, the immediate need is for $250,000 of incremental funding to sustain the program through the remainder of the year."

[*Rationale*] "If we do not invest this incremental spending now, we will end up with expensive fire drills, erosion of customer confidence, and inevitably, bad press."

[*Example*] "As you know, scrutiny of cost and schedule performance in our industry continues to increase and past performance influences future business awards. We cannot afford to fail, especially as we start to enter into production."

[*Key Points*] "In today's meeting, we'll cover three things: P&L impact, supplier management, and resource allocation."

[*Check-In*] "Does that make sense?"

Key Point 1 P&L Impact	Key Point 2 Supplier Management	Key Point 3 Resource Allocation
Sub-point 1 Deliveries substantially increase in two years.	Sub-point 1 Supplier has responded well to our advice and coaching.	Sub-point 1 We have highly competent and engaged team on both sides.
Sub-point 2 We can't dial up production quickly. Lead times are well over eight months with a delivery rate of one set of parts every six weeks.	Sub-point 2 Regular presence and frequent communication build trust and honesty into our interactions, and promote improved performance.	Sub-point 2 Program interruptions will result in resources moving to other assignments and limit future availability.
Sub-point 3 This item is on the critical path with no schedule slack. Interruptions end up with day-to-day slips.	Sub-point 3 Disengagement sends the wrong message, especially since everyone knows the job isn't finished yet.	Sub-point 3 Necessary supplier investments supporting us may be reprioritized.

[*Closing*] "Next steps are to brief the program on this need and discuss options for funding resources."

Outcome: Following the actual meeting with senior management, Bill let us know that Tony managed to get his message across, and there was a search for the resources needed to complete the project. Bill felt that "it may not be a win, but at least it will be hard to say no." Sometimes the path to victory is taken in baby steps.

Example: Starting Employee Resource Groups

Background: Vice President of Human Resources Corporate for Stanley Black & Decker Jo Yarranton is a champion of diversity and inclusion within her organization. She is one of the founders of Global Women's Network at the company. Through her team's leadership, Stanley Black & Decker launched its first Employee Resource Group (ERG) in 2015. The African Ancestry group came next. At the time of this writing (2019), the organization's diversity and inclusion initiative has grown to nine active ERGs. It's easy to look at this success and think, "That was easy." But it was bloody hard work, based on many important discussions, decisions, and actions.

We asked Yarranton if she could reconstruct the critical meeting where she got executive approval to launch the Women's Network. We gave her the PARE Strategy and Building Blocks Methodology worksheets and asked her to fill them out in a way that modeled what actually happened in that successful meeting. Here is what she sent back to us. We wanted to include this example in the book because some of you might be facing a similar opportunity in your organization. Having Jo's plan for facilitating a successful discussion on women's leadership development and diversity in the workplace may be of value to you and your organization. Enjoy!

[*Topic and Context*] "We are here to talk about establishing a Global Women's Network at Stanley Black & Decker. Why now? Recent talent hires have led to a natural cohort of high-achieving women. We wish to harness this talent globally to develop others."

[*Position*] "We believe that we need to create an environment where women are empowered to grow and succeed at Stanley Black & Decker."

[*Ask*] "We want you to approve the creation of the Global Women's Network and to provide executive sponsorship."

[*Rationale*] "If you agree, you will help us attract and retain more high-performing women and increase our employer brand reputation. If you don't agree, we will continue to bear the high costs of turnover and lost opportunities."

[*Example*] "A study by Korn Ferry Institute estimated an annual cost to American employers of $64 billion dollars in employee turnover—plus additional costs around diminished morale, decreased sales, and limited talent pools—all stemming from the failure to effectively manage diversity in the workplace."

[*Key Points*] "Today, we will cover three things related to the formation of the Global Women's Network: P&L impact, strategy, and benefits."

[*Check-In*] "Let's take a look at the numbers first."

Key Point 1	Key Point 2	Key Point 3
P&L Impact	**Strategy**	**Benefits**
Sub-point 1	**Sub-point 1**	**Sub-point 1**
Money saved from reduced attrition of female employees — Lori's story	Build bench strength of diverse talent through new development initiatives — Programming examples	Positive impact on our employer brand on review sites like Glassdoor — Show screenshots
Sub-point 2	**Sub-point 2**	**Sub-point 2**
Reduced search fees with the recent increase in external referrals of female talent — Show chart with savings	Role and selection of the new Executive Sponsor	Internal and external energy around the creation of additional ERGs
Sub-point 3	**Sub-point 3**	**Sub-point 3**
Exposure for emerging females assigned to new roles—Two specific examples	Map formation and pipeline to creation of other ERGs including African Ancestry	Inclusion in Best Places to Work surveys referencing diversity and women's empowerment

[*Closing*] "Lori and I will finalize the framework of the Global Women's Network with a target launch date of October 2015. We will report back results at the next board meeting. Thank you."

Outcome: As you know, Jo was successful at this meeting with the executive team. She got her desired outcome—agreement to establish the company's Global Women's Network. But she got so much more than just that. In her own words: "Success is taking one idea, thinking it through and formulating a plan. I would never have believed that having a group of like-minded women come together would lead to nine Employee Resource Groups in less than three years. We changed the course of diversity and inclusion at Stanley Black & Decker." It's very motivating to see what can happen when we effectively and efficiently facilitate discussions that lead to action and positive change.

Example: Special Assessment for Office Park Signage

Background: One of our clients is in the commercial investment and property management industry. She was preparing for an important discussion at the Property Owners Association (POA) annual meeting. In preparation for this meeting, she and her subcommittee were asked to lead a discussion on improving the signage at one of their professional office parks. After many weeks of research and exploration, she and her team were ready to make a recommendation to the owners' group. They would need a two-thirds vote to pass the motion for a special assessment to invest in new signage. She would be asking for unbudgeted money and she was nervous. To get ready, she and her committee worked through the PARE Strategy and Building Blocks Methodology worksheets. They decided how they were going to frame the discussion, what information was germane to the discussion and decision, and what information was unnecessary detail and noise. Two of the owners would be joining the meeting via conference call (audio only), while the other four owners would be physically in the meeting room. Below is the discussion game plan:

[*Topic and Context*] "Our main agenda item is the signage improvement project. As you know, our professional office park is over twenty years old, and while the buildings still look good, the signage is old and tired."

[*Position*] "We believe that we need to invest in improving our signage to remain competitive in the market for leasing commercial office space in our area."

[*Ask*] "We are asking the POA board to approve a special assessment to fund modernization of signage at our office park."

[*Rationale*] "If we do this, we will keep our current tenants satisfied and attract new tenants and buyers. If you don't improve signage, it will take longer to fill vacancies and sell buildings."

[*Example*] "Our recent tenant survey on the signage revealed that the majority are very dissatisfied with the current pylon sign, stating that it is 'inadequate,' 'useless,' 'cluttered,' 'dated,' and 'not eye-catching.'"

[*Key Points*] "In our discussion today, we'd like to cover three things: The pylon sign, monument signs, and next steps."

[*Check-In*] "Ready to dive in?"

Key Point 1 Pylon Sign	Key Point 2 Monument Sign	Key Point 3 Next Steps
Sub-point 1 Recommended changes: - LED electronic color board - New covering on structure - Updated branding	**Sub-point 1** Recommended plan: - Keep brick structures - Refresh all signs - Update colors/style/ font - Allow tenants to use their brand logos	**Sub-point 1** Motion to approve special assessment of $95,000 for signage improvement - Official vote (Note: Have contingency plan at the ready)
Sub-point 2 Investment - Quotes from two vendors - Range $65,000 - 85,000 - Costs to operate	**Sub-point 2** Investment - Estimated cost to implement $5,000-$10,000	**Sub-point 2** Vendor Selection - Negotiations - Contracting and deposit - Financing options
Sub-point 3 Benefits - Modern & eye catching - High visibility for traffic - Highlight tenant brands - Revenue opportunity for specials and advertising	**Sub-point 3** Other Signage - Placards: set standards for placement - Show placard designs used by competition - Window signs—discourage	**Sub-point 3** Implementation Plan - Design phase and approvals - Roll out first with Monument signs and placards - Tenant communication - Installation

[*Closing*] "The motion carries. The signage improvement project is approved. Thank you for investing in our professional office park and ensuring that it remains competitive for many years to come."

Outcome: The motion was passed with one hundred percent approval by the POA board. Surprisingly, there were no dissenting votes. Our client reported that as each key point was discussed, there was open and respectful communication. This helped to build trust and understanding. No one was trying to "hard sell" or "railroad" anybody. One of the subcommittee members did an excellent job of securing agreement to each section before moving on to the next key point.

Our client also shared with us that she deliberately did not mention the exact amount she would be asking for until after the discussion. "We didn't want to shock them or put them on the defensive at the very beginning. When it became clear that they were excited about this change and very open to and eager to make an investment in the professional office park, she decided to make a motion on the high side of the vendors' quotes."

She also told us that they walked away knowing more about the other members of the POA board and felt more positive about future discussions and collaborations. Yes indeed, facilitating productive discussions has the potential for many positive outcomes.

Practice Makes Permanent

As you have experienced in prior chapters, we believe it is important that you apply what you have learned in order to truly understand how it works. But we don't want to bore you with topics that we have already gone over a few times. So, we are going to throw you a new scenario—one that might be useful in your life.

Your mission, should you choose to accept it, is to create a hypothetical PARE opening and a Building Blocks Methodology outline for one of these important discussions (select one):

1. Asking your manager for a promotion, a raise in pay, or a stretch assignment

2. Discussing with your significant partner the idea of taking a vacation together

Fill in the blanks.

[Topic and Context]

_____

_____

[Position]

_____

_____

[Ask]

_____

_____

[Rationale]

_____

_____

[Example]

_____

_____

[*Key Points*]

1. _____ 2. _____ 3. _____

[*Check-In*]

_____

_____

Key Point 1	Key Point 2	Key Point 3
_____	_____	_____
Sub-point 1	Sub-point 1	Sub-point 1
_____	_____	_____
_____	_____	_____
_____	_____	_____
Sub-point 2	Sub-point 2	Sub-point 2
_____	_____	_____
_____	_____	_____
_____	_____	_____
Sub-point 3	Sub-point 3	Sub-point 3
_____	_____	_____
_____	_____	_____
_____	_____	_____

[*Closing*]

_____

_____

Contingency Planning

When preparing for your discussion, you must develop a Plan A and a Plan B version. Think of Plan A as the perfect scenario in which everything goes according to plan. You frame the discussion with your brilliant and brief PARE Strategy opening; you present just enough data to support your point of view; you get their agreement, close the meeting, and *voila*, once again you have proven that you are an amazing communicator.

But how often does that happen? Maybe 5-10 percent of the time?

That's why you need a Plan B: a contingency plan that prepares you for the inevitable. Because communication is a two-way street, your listeners will naturally have questions and comments, and occasionally a zinger or two that they want to throw at you just to see how you handle it. In chapter 11, we will give you a strategy to handle those interruptions without losing your cool. It is imperative that you be able to answer those questions with respect and calmness. And you must find your way back to Plan A as quickly as possible. Never wing it; always come prepared with both a Plan A and a Plan B.

Without further ado, let's get you ready for the hot seat.

Chapter 11

Aikido For Challenges

You've just read about how to structure your message and discussion so that you're clear, organized, and concise. You use the Building Blocks Methodology to map everything out, put together clear slides, and plan a flawless discussion or presentation with no interruptions, challenges, or detours. And how often does that happen? Very rarely, if ever. You have to have a plan for the challenges, the detours, the interruptions.

Imagine a spouse was sitting in her kitchen, cleaning up dishes after dinner as she and her husband began talking with one another.

Husband: "Why are you washing the pots?"

Spouse: "Um, because they're dirty?"

Husband: "Yeah, but why are you washing them?"

Spouse: (*Getting more annoyed*) "Because they're dirty."

Husband: "OK, but why are you washing them?"

Spouse: (*Definitely annoyed*) "Because someone has to."

Husband: "You don't have to."

Spouse: (*Beyond annoyed*) "Really? Because I don't see you washing them."

Husband: (*Also becoming annoyed*) "Well, I was asking because I usually wash the pots. That's why I was asking why *you* were washing them."

This is a classic example of what is known as an attack-defend spiral. Master negotiators have coined this phrase to describe what can happen when others push back or challenge us in some real or imagined way.

Sometimes, a listener will—intentionally or unintentionally—ask a question or say something to throw you off. We call that an *attack communication behavior*. Most of us will then default to some sort of defense with a *defend communication behavior*.

That defend communication behavior leads to another attack communication behavior, which leads to another defend communication, behavior, and so on. The communication spirals downward, like an auguring tool. This is not a good place to be and it's often hard to recover from.

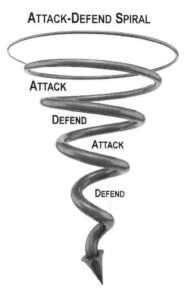

ATTACK-DEFEND SPIRAL

Attack behavior followed by a...

Defend behavior followed by an...

ATTACK

Attack behavior followed by a...

DEFEND

Defend behavior followed by an...

ATTACK

Attack behavior followed by a...

DEFEND

Defend behavior followed by an...

Attack behavior followed by a...

Aikido is the exact opposite of attack-defend behaviors. Founded by Morihei Ueshiba, the American Aikido Association (AAA) describes aikido as a martial art that focuses on harmonizing with your opponent to bring peaceful resolutions to situations involving conflict.

> *"To injure an opponent is to injure yourself. To control aggression without inflicting injury is the Art of Peace."*
>
> —Morihei Ueshiba

So, the question becomes, how do we stop our natural tendency to want to defend when we feel we are being attacked? You have to change your communication behavior using one of these two methods:

1. Attack behavior followed by a seeking behavior

2. Attack behavior followed by a summarizing behavior

But, how can you do this? As you know, we are fanatics for efficiency, and having a strategy for this is critical. We've got one. It's called *Handling A Challenge*.

The Idea In Brief

Handling A Challenge

Use a simple, five-step process to help you *respond* and not simply *react* to a question or statement when you feel the need to defend.

STEP 1 ▶ *If necessary, press for specifics*

STEP 2 ▶ *Paraphrase the challenger's point of view or feeling*

STEP 3 ▶ *Respond with key points, facts, support, or data*

STEP 4 ▶ *Check in*

STEP 5 ▶ *Reconnect*

Let's look at each of the steps in more detail.

The Five Steps Of Handling A Challenge

STEP 1: *If Necessary, Press For Specifics*

This sounds like, "What do you mean by...?" or "Say more about that..." or "What specifically is unclear/concerns you?" This is a *seeking behavior*.

It's easy for us to simply want to jump in and say something—anything—even when the person asking a question or challenging us in some way isn't completely clear. The authors have seen this time and time again. For example, someone might say, "I don't get it. The numbers aren't adding up." Wild Bores immediately start to provide data, or explain how they got to a calculation, or assume they know which numbers the person is talking about. They make assumptions, and this, in turn, leads us straight into an attack-defend spiral.

STEP 2: *Paraphrase The Challenger's Point Of View Or Feeling*

This sounds like: "So you're concerned because..." or "Let me make sure I'm tracking with you. You're saying that..." This is a *summarizing behavior*.

Clearly, you don't want to do this if the question or challenge is straightforward. For example, "Who else was on the project with you?" It would sound contrived and, frankly, silly to respond with "So you want to know who else was on the project with me." Duh. But if you're dealing with challenges to what you are saying, proposing, or presenting, this step is mission-critical.

Let's demonstrate with an example that would be appropriate. Let's say you get a challenge like this:

- "Are you kidding me? We've spent three years, I don't know how much money, and a whole lot of time on this system, not to mention resources. Now you're telling me that we need to revisit phase two of the project?"

A step-two paraphrasing response might be: "You're concerned because you feel like our proposal will bring us right back to where we started and might not make a difference. Is that right?"

If you do step two correctly, the challenger will likely give some affirmation—a verbal "Yes," or "You got it," or "Uh huh." Or it may be a nonverbal affirmation in the form of a nod. Either way, getting this affirmation is crucial to avoiding attack-defend spirals. It shows the challenger that you heard them clearly or accurately. And it also allows them to be in a place to listen to your response or answer. People can't buy in until they have weighed in. Don't *tell* someone you heard them; *show* them by paraphrasing.

"People can't buy in until they've weighed in."

STEP 3: *Respond With Key Points, Facts, Support, Or Data*

This sounds like: "When we did our analysis on this project, we found we only used half of our allocated budget. That means we still have enough time and resources to complete the project on time, with quality."

The trick to this step is to be brief, be brilliant, and be done. If you over-talk the answer or response, you will end up rambling, providing information that may have nothing to do with the challenge or question, or start contradicting yourself. You will sound out-of-control and give others the opportunity to poke holes or challenge something unrelated to the point you want to make. Say what you need to say, base it on a point or data that you've already made, and be quiet.

"Be Brief. Be Brilliant. Be Done."

STEP 4: *Check In*

This sounds like, "Does that clarify it?" or "Make sense?" or "Ready to move on?" and is a simple but important step. There are several benefits to checking in:

- You will know whether or not you were clear.

- You'll know whether you need to clarify a key point, or provide additional data, facts, or support.

- You'll get affirmation that the person is satisfied and ready to move on.

- It puts you back into control of the discussion.

Step 5: Reconnect To The Point You Were Making (Or Where You May Need To Go Next)

This sounds like, "So we were discussing..." or "So based on that, let's take a look at the data now..."

It may be that you'll need to jump ahead or go back or simply move forward from where you were. It doesn't matter, because you are, once again, taking control of the discussion.

Putting It All Together

Here are some examples of how the steps for *Handling A Challenge* could work. These examples are modified from challenges that we have heard or have gotten ourselves.

Example: Using Storytelling in Presentations

[*Challenger*] "This makes no sense."

[*Step 1*] "What's unclear?"

[*Challenger*] "Storytelling is all the rage. I get it. It seems good in theory, but I don't really see how people can use this when they present. Most people can't tell a good story to save their lives and if they start doing this in the middle of an important presentation, they are going to lose all credibility."

[*Step 2*] "So you don't want to have speakers do something in their presentations that they can't do well and impact their reputation with the senior team. Do I have that right?"

[*Challenger*] "Exactly. These presenters are nervous enough and we want to make sure that the senior leaders see them as having potential to take on greater levels of responsibility."

[*Step 3*] "There may be times when storytelling isn't an appropriate thing to do. What we are recommending is that people in our program practice using this skill so they can use it naturally and appropriately to build their credibility. As I stated earlier, Gallup identified the ability to tell and connect stories as one of the biggest communication differentiators in leaders."

[*Step 4*] "Does that make sense?"

[*Challenger*] "I suppose so. I'd like to hear more about how you teach people how to do this."

[*Step 5*] "Great. Let's talk about the storytelling structure and methods and how to use this in presentations and we can come back to our training implementation plan."

Example: Leadership Development Training

[*Challenger*] "We've already looked at the feasibility of having people attend training for a full day. I can't see how this is going to work."

[*Step 1*] *None needed. This is pretty clear.*

[*Step 2*] "So you're mostly concerned about how to make this happen given time and budget constraints."

[*Challenger*] "Yes, exactly. And, frankly, I don't think people have the attention span to sit for a full day."

[*Step 3*] "Actually, we anticipated that timing was going to be a concern. We have two options for this. First, we looked at everyone's schedules and determined full-day dates that were best for everyone. Second, we could split the sessions up into two half-day sessions to ensure the most flexible schedule possible.

[*Step 4*] "Does that help with your concerns?"

[*Challenger*] "Absolutely."

[*Step 5*] "OK. Let's talk more about the timetable and then get back to the content and what folks will be doing. I think that will address your concern about participant focus."

Example 3: Using PARE Strategy

[*Challenger*] "I don't get it."

[*Step 1*] "What do you mean?"

[*Challenger*] "The PARE Strategy approach seems like overkill. I mean, come on. If I'm updating my boss, you really expect me to talk about what will happen if they don't do what I'm asking? This is my boss I'm talking about. He's not going to like to be told what to do. He's the one calling the shots; I'm just doing an update."

[*Step 2*] "You're thinking that the PARE Strategy might be a bit too much in the context of a simple update to your boss," or, "So you're not sure if using a PARE opening in an update meeting applies to your world."

[*Challenger*] *(Nods his head)*

[Step 3] "You're right. There are times when using the entire strategy doesn't make sense, especially for something simple. That's why we are going to talk about when and how to modify and use parts of the strategy that would be most relevant in a given situation."

[*Step 4*] "Does that explanation help?"

[*Challenger*] "Yes, it does."

[*Step 5*] "We are going to be talking about how to make modifications to the PARE Strategy in about fifteen minutes. First, I'd like to talk about other communication strategies critical for influencing."

Five Steps For Handling A Challenge

1. Don't skip steps. Unless you understand the challenge and don't need to press for specifics, follow the steps. If you skip (especially Step 2 summarizing) you will immediately be in the attack-defend spiral.

2. Take your time. Make sure you know *exactly* what the issue is before you summarize or paraphrase your understanding.

3. Be quiet. After you summarize or paraphrase at Step 2, *pause*. Wait for the affirmation to come and *then* give your answer. Otherwise, you will be perceived as someone who is just waiting to talk, not someone who is listening.

4. Change up Step 4. We all get into verbal habits and it's easy to keep using the same check-in phrase. "Doesn't that make sense? Make sense? Making sense?" Try some others, like:

   - "Good?"
   - "Does that help clear it up?"
   - "Does that help with your concerns?"
   - "Does that answer your question?"
   - "Ready to move on?"

5. Work with what's presented to you, not against it. That's the essence of aikido and the way to get out of the attack-defend spiral.

Practice Makes Permanent

Again, we are convinced of the power of practice. And practicing a bit of verbal aikido when dealing with challenges is the best way to make this strategy effortless.

Think about some possible challenges or pushback that you might encounter during your discussion. Below, write exactly what that would sound like, giving as much information as possible. Write it as if the challenger were actually speaking to you.

My challenge would sound like:

"
_____
_____
_____ "

Now, write what you would say to demonstrate each of the steps in _Handling A Challenge._

1. If necessary, press for specifics.

    _____
    _____
    _____
    _____

2. Paraphrase or summarize the challenger's point of view or feeling.

    _____
    _____
    _____
    _____

3. Respond with key points, facts, support, and/or data.

_____
_____
_____
_____

4. Check in with the challenger.

_____
_____
_____
_____

5. Reconnect to a point you were making.

_____
_____
_____
_____

Congratulations! If you've done all of the activities in this book, we are confident you are on your way to slaying the Wild Bore. And to be sure the Wild Bore is buried for good, we have some techniques and strategies to make sure that all that you've practiced does, indeed, become permanent.

Read on to see how.

Chapter 12

Go Further

You now have new strategies, skills, and insight to help you win the battle for communication efficiency. By consistently applying the tools in this book, you will develop a reputation for being both an efficient and effective communicator. But be forewarned, as Wild Bores are pervasive. They roam freely in your organization, in your social circles, and in your community. The Wild Bore instincts also remain dormant deep inside each of us. We must remain vigilant and keep the Wild Bore at bay. How can we do this? That is focus of this final chapter.

Practice With These Coaching Questions

If you freeze up or blank out during any part of your PARE Strategy opening, try using some of these in-the-moment coaching tips to remind you of what comes next. Attention managers: these coaching questions work beautifully to help you guide your direct reports as they formulate a PARE opening on any topic for the first time. Each point of the PARE Strategy can be prompted by a question:

1. So, what are we talking about today? [*Topic*]

2. Why? Why are we talking about this now? [*Context*]

3. What do you think, feel or believe? [*Position*]

4. So, what do you want me to do exactly? [*Ask*]

5. Why should I? or, What might happen if I don't? [*Rationale*]

6. Do you have any evidence for this? [*Example*]

7. So, what are we going to be talking about next? [*Key Points*]

8. Gently prompt them, "Remember to check in." [*Check In*]

Confidence Building

The PARE Strategy has other powerful effects including increased confidence and courage. The more you work with the PARE Strategy, the more you will know your content. You will be able to open the discussion "naked" (by that, we mean free of notes and boring slides). No more relying on PowerPoint slides to remind you of what you want to say next. No more hanging on to index cards, cheat sheets, or your digital device to give you a sense of security. The truth is that these crutches only result in distracting your audience and diminishing your impact.

Steve Jobs, cofounder of the Apple organization and mastermind behind this iconic brand, was famous for saying, "People who know what they are talking about don't need PowerPoint." Legend has it that Steve became so sick and tired of sitting in internal meetings where people "presented" to each other rather than having meaningful discussions, that he outlawed PowerPoint in all meetings. We think Steve would have loved the PARE Strategy.

"People who know what they are talking about don't need PowerPoint."

— Steve Jobs

The more you work with the PARE Strategy, the more you will find yourself able to open discussions with no notes, and no slides— at least, not in the first ninety seconds of the discussion, when it matters most.

Dial It Up

Here are six final steps to help you practice and perfect your opening using the PARE Strategy.

1. Write it down. For each part of your opening, write down what you will say. You can script it longhand or use the PARE Strategy worksheet. Then, read it out loud at least five times.

2. Try it with no notes. It doesn't matter if you don't say exactly what's on your worksheet. Just understand the flow and concentrate on being clear and efficient with each PARE Strategy component.

3. Slow down. Briefly pause between each sentence. Speeding through your opening is a ticketable offense. We want you to be brief in your communication, but we don't want you to rush.

4. Time it. Use the stopwatch feature on your digital device. Remember, don't rush. If you are efficient in your words, your opening should take less than ninety seconds to communicate verbally.

5. Do mirror work. Practice your opening using the PARE Strategy in front of the mirror. There's a good reason the technique is used by many great actors and performers; it works!

6. Get real—people, that is. Get real people to listen to you when you practice or dress-rehearse. Don't just do it in your head. Choose whether to stand up or sit down—whichever aligns with how you'll actually be facilitating the discussion.

Play The Game

A fun way to master the PARE Strategy is to play the game, *Give Me A Topic, Any Topic.* You can play the game by yourself or with other people. *Give Me A Topic, Any Topic* will help build your familiarity with the PARE Strategy and allow you to call upon it when you need it. For example, when you are asked to lead a discussion at the last minute, you'll be better able to think on your feet.

Give Me A Topic, Any Topic.

This game is meant to be playful. You will be asked to quickly formulate a PARE opening on an arbitrary topic suggested by someone else. In this game, you are allowed to make up some context and content so that you can perform on the spot. But we caution not to use this game to formulate viewpoints or try to unduly influence others on topics that you have not fully researched or thought about.

Here's where and when you can play the game *Give Me A Topic, Any Topic*:

Setting 1: Self-Study. While listening to or reading local or world news, think about the topic being reported by the journalist for a few minutes. Now turn off the radio, put down the newspaper, or flip over your tablet so you are not distracted by the media. In your mind's eye, call up the PARE Strategy and begin to prepare responses for each of the steps, all the way through the check-in. Verbalize out loud your hypothetical opening for this particular topic. It doesn't have to be perfect or even accurate; it's just important that you follow all the steps in the PARE Strategy. Allow yourself to smile, chuckle, or laugh. It's just practice.

Setting 2: Team-Building Exercise. After your team is introduced to the Sharpening Your Point process by reading this book or completing the training course, you can reinforce your team's learning and have fun at the same time. At the start of each team meeting, play *Give Me a Topic, Any Topic*, as an icebreaker. Ask for a volunteer or rotate to a new team member at each meeting until everyone has had their turn in the hot seat. You are allowed one free pass in which you can ask for a different topic. We suggest you ask for an "easy" topic, avoiding sensitive topics such as politics, religion, or sex. You can use this game as an interactive exercise during an offsite meeting. Split the group into teams of three or four people and have them practice formulating openings using the PARE Strategy within their subgroups.

Setting 3: Social Settings. Show off your knowledge and impromptu ability by asking your friends to *Give Me A Topic, Any Topic* during social mixers or dinner parties. They will be amazed at how quick you are on your feet. Warning: don't overdo this, as they might begin to think of you as an annoying Wild Bore.

Special Challenges

The tools and strategies of the Sharpening Your Point process can also be effective in other situations. Here are three examples provided to us by clients:

Communicating Up. If you struggle with the best way to provide status updates to your boss, you should consider using the PARE Strategy and Building Blocks Methodology. One of our clients was having trouble pinning down her boss for update meetings. The boss was traveling a lot and was in the office only infrequently. Our client had to resort to communicating updates to her manager via email, and he would often complain that her emails were "too long." Their different communication styles and technology preferences were started to erode their relationship. The solution? Our client used the Sharpening Your Point process to structure more effective status updates with her boss. Even when she couldn't be face-to-face with him, she was able to communicate the essential information in a timely and efficient manner. Best of all, she learned to state her position and make an ask in every update. This helped position our client as a leader, not just a reporter of information.

Presentation Opening Remarks. It's important to know exactly what you are going to say when you open your presentation so that you can grab the attention of your audience. One of our clients who is a Vistage Chair and facilitates CEO roundtables had great success in using the PARE Strategy as part of his opening remarks. In fact, he created a two-part presentation opener: First, he started with a personal story about a former Vistage member, then he elegantly moved into the PARE Strategy to frame the important discussion that they were going to have that day. It was a brilliant combination and worked like magic to captivate and hold the attention of the busy CEOs in the room.

New Spin to the Meeting Notice. Another client had the great idea to use selected parts of the Sharpening Your Point process to issue more useful meeting notices. Rather than some obscure calendar invitation with limited information, she began to use elements of the PARE

Strategy to provide more context for the discussion and motivation to attend the meeting. While our client didn't share all the elements of the PARE Strategy in the meeting notice, she did share:

- Topic and context

- Key points to be discussed

Spotting Wild Bores In Social Settings

Perhaps it's easiest to spot a Wild Bore in a social setting. That's where they feel most at home, free of the pressure to adhere to professional standards of communication. And so, they just let loose, speaking endlessly, without ever making a point. And they wonder why people look around the room to see who else is available. It's not rudeness, it's basic survival.

The more you study the art of communication efficiency, the more often you will recognize its opposite. We invite you to observe, without judgement, situations of communication inefficiency in action. Notice what's happening and not happening. Watch the reaction of other people who are the victims of these Wild Bores. In effect, they are a captured audience, bound by social pressure to be polite and listen. From a safe vantage point, you can observe their attempts to pivot the conversation by injecting a question or introducing a new topic. Notice how the Wild Bore appears to be in their own world, deaf to the listener's silent plea to "Get to the Point!"

My Point Is...

The sentence-starter, "My point is…," is one of the most focusing phrases you can say in a conversation. It not only wakes up your listeners, but it helps you, as the communicator, remember your main job: to make a relevant point. And the PARE Strategy and Building Blocks Methodology help you do just that.

It doesn't matter if you are in a social or a professional setting; you owe it to yourself and the people around you to sharpen your point and to get to the point as quickly as possible. Life is short. Your sentences should be too.

So, here's a new mantra that you need to add to your favorites: *My point is_____.*

Remember to fill in the blank whenever you find yourself being taken over by your own Wild Bore. Making the point will drive the Wild Bore away and keep you on good terms with your friends, boss, and customers.

Visualization To The Rescue

What happens if you are so nervous before the meeting or discussion that you freeze up and totally forget what you were going to say? No worries. You can train your brain to remember the framework of the PARE Strategy and recall it even during times of stress (such as during an important meeting, discussion, or public presentation). To prove this point, we reached out to an expert in the field of neuroscience.

John Medina is a developmental molecular biologist (aka brainyologist) and is an in-demand speaker on the topic of neuroscience and how our brains work. He is an affiliate professor at the University of Washington School of Medicine and the author of one of our favorite books on the topic: *Brain Rules: 12 Principles for Surviving and Thriving at Work, Home, and School.*[6] You can see Medina in action on his YouTube channel: https://www.youtube.com/user/brainrulesbook.

---

[6] John Medina, *Brain Rules: 12 Principles for Surviving and Thriving at Work, Home and School.* Pear Press, 2014.

Medina told us that one of the ways in which you can help your brain remember something like the PARE Strategy and be able to recall it when you need it is to encode it: not just any old encoding, but elaborate and deep encoding—that's the key to making stronger memories. There are three types of encoding:

- Semantic encoding (paying attention to the definition of words)

- Phonemic encoding (paying attention to the sounds)

- Structural encoding (visual inspection of shapes)

Medina believes that it is this last type of encoding, the structural encoding, that allows a given piece of information to enter your head in a way that increases your ability to remember the information at a later date.

First of all, take out your smartphone or digital device and take a picture of the PARE Strategy worksheet on the opposing page. Save it as a favorite. This is the image that we want you to store in your long-term memory. We have found that if you pull up this image in your mind's eye, you can create a PARE Strategy opening anywhere, anytime.

To lock that image in and help your brain even more, Medina suggests the following fun-filled visualization exercise to aid your memory and comprehension:

Close your eyes. Allow a slow, deep breath to relax you. Now, imagine your body is shrunk down to a teeny, tiny size. Imagine that in front of you is an equally small, passenger drone of your own design. It's safe, autonomous, lightweight, and super cool. Can you picture that? This is the perfect vehicle for your reconnaissance mission. You have been tasked to obtain information by visual observation or other detection methods about a new thing called the PARE Strategy that is appearing in the sky over your workplace. You, in your drone, carefully lift off and approach the PARE image from the right side, taking photos with the drone's onboard imaging capabilities. Then you move to the opposite side to capture images from another angle. You move behind it, above it, underneath it, at different angles, all the while capturing the images that you will take home to your team so that they can ascertain the threat that this PARE phenomena might pose to the safety and security of Wild Bores everywhere. Once you are satisfied that you have photographed, observed, and measured the PARE object from every possible angle, you return home to the base. You shut down the drone, and safely step out of your tiny aircraft. As you open your eyes, you magically return to normal physical size. And then you open your eyes and come back to now.

What Just Happened?

According to Medina, you just anchored the PARE Strategy framework into your brain using structural encoding. You enhanced the pattern-matching aspect of the PARE Strategy in a way that will help your brain encode, store, and retrieve the information. It's not enough to memorize information or even to look at an image as just a square. You have to see it from different angles and directions. Visualization helps the brain to remember what you've learned. And

PARE Strategy

Topic What?	Context Statement Why Now?

Position
I think, believe, feel

Ask
I want you to …

Rationale
If you do …
If you don't …

Example
We know this because…

Key Point # 1	Key Point # 2	Key Point # 3

Check in with Audience

we want you to remember, recall, and use the PARE Strategy to open your discussions.

The Most Important Single Factor

According to Medina, "If you are trying to get information across to someone, your ability to create a compelling introduction may be the most important single factor in the later success of your mission."

As we wrap up Part 3 of this book, we want to leave you with one last thought: You can be brief and compelling at the same time. As is often the case, the more words you use, the less compelling you are, and the quicker you will lose your listener's attention. The PARE Strategy allows you to open the discussion in a concise and compelling way. And that's vital to your success.

> *"If you are trying to get information across to someone, your ability to create a compelling introduction may be the most important single factor in the later success of your mission."*
>
> —Dr. John Medina, author of *Brain Rules*

Drone At The Ready

We also want you to structurally encode the Building Blocks Methodology into your brain for easier recall. So, it's time to shrink down again, get into your imaginary mini drone, and buzz all around the image of the Building Blocks Methodology worksheet on the following page. We want you to see this helpful framework in your mind's eye and refer to it whenever you are preparing to lead a discussion or a presentation. So, fuel up your mini-drone. It's time for another flight.

The Building Blocks Methodology

OPENING (Use the PARE Strategy)

Provide Relevant Details For Each Key Point

Key Point 1	Key Point 2	Key Point 3

Sub-Point 1	Sub-Point 1	Sub-Point 1

Sub-Point 2	Sub-Point 2	Sub-Point 2

Sub-Point 3	Sub-Point 3	Sub-Point 3

CLOSING (Try the WWW closing – *Who does What by When*)

Tools At The Ready

One of the best ways to prevent yourself from slipping back into the bad habits of a Wild Bore is to use the tools provided in this book. To make that easier for you, we have converted them into writable PDF formats, which you can download and use for any meeting, discussion, or presentation. This PDF format will allow you to use your laptop or digital device to develop the outline for your upcoming discussion.

We also have clients who like to print out the worksheets and use colored sticky notes to write down their content. Since the sticky notes are small, you are forced to be brief and to the point. Plus, you can easily change the order of your content by moving the sticky notes around (e.g., you decided that you want to switch the order between Key Point 1 and Key Point 2).

Lastly, some clients like to write out their opening using the PARE Strategy in full sentence form. Whatever way works best for you, the key is to move these tools out of this book and into your work life. Do this now, by downloading the PDF formats at:

http://www. sharpeningyourpoint.com. The password is Sharpen.

Winning The Battle For Communication Efficiency

By now, you realize this book is not about storytelling; it's about communication efficiency. This is important because people today are seriously distracted and have very short attention spans.

We believe that it's your job to sharpen your point and say only what you mean when facilitating discussions.

Thousands of professionals have shared their challenges and successes with us. It's an ongoing battle for communication efficiency.

We want you to not only use the tools and strategies contained in this book, but also to share them with your colleagues and friends. Help us spread the word.

If you do this, you'll increase your impact at work and develop a reputation as a skilled communicator.

Imagine a world where people say what they mean clearly and concisely. Imagine a workplace where you can use fewer words and have more impact and greater influence. It's time to slay the Wild Bore.

Here's to your success!

Resources – Leesa Wallace

- Talk to Leesa about her proven method for building a better leader—The Leadership Academy. This longer-term development program is not a check-the-box, but a change-behavior initiative that has helped hundreds of future and current leaders act more strategically, think more deeply, and listen more powerfully.

- Hire Leesa to facilitate any of her signature programs, such as *Coaching For Performance and Engagement*, *Building Productive Relationships*, *Leading From The Middle*, *Cool Under Pressure*, *Situational Leadership*, *Making Meetings Matter*, *Turning Lecture Into Learning*, *Performance Consulting*, and *Leading High Performing Teams*.

- To help get you ready for that high-stakes presentation, hire Leesa as your executive presentation skills coach. Her coaching method and techniques are described as transformative and powerful.

- Book Leesa as a keynote speaker for an upcoming conference, leadership meeting, or lunch and learn.

- Is one of your teams not working the way it should? Let Leesa diagnose, consult, and develop a path to getting the group focused and working more effectively.

Resources – Kathy McAfee

- Talk with Kathy about her signature program, *The Motivated Presenter* coaching and training series, and how it can help you and your team be better prepared, more engaging, and have greater impact in your presentations and meetings. The series is available in a variety of formats, including two-day intensive workshop, one-day mastery class, half-day program, one-on-one coaching, team coaching, webinar series, and as a *Lunch-and-Lead Motivating Seminar*.

- Hire Kathy or Leesa to facilitate a half-day or full-day *Sharpening Your Point* training program for your team.

- Book Kathy as the keynote speaker for your next corporate meeting, professional conference, or industry association event. Her topics include communication, networking, and personal branding.

- Need an external speaker or breakout facilitator to dial up the impact for employee resource groups (e.g., women's network, young professional network, etc.) that are part of your diversity and inclusion initiatives? This is an area of true passion and experience for Kathy. She'll help you strategize and get more creative on how to power up your ERG programming.

- Need someone to help you smooth out your rough edges and hold you accountable to your goals? Hire Kathy as your executive coach. Virtual coaching makes it more convenient to get the help you need when you need it.

- Need a dose of inspiration to keep you engaged at work? Read Kathy's blog or sign up to receive her newsletter: *Elevate: Take Your Talent to the Next Level.* https://www.americasmarketingmotivator.com/#signup

Acknowledgments

Leesa Wallace

I would not be where I am today, doing what I love, without the wisdom, guidance and support of my music teacher, Karen Haines. She gave me far more than a love for music. She believed in my abilities, kept me focused on the right things, and took me to task when I needed it the most. She changed the trajectory of my life, and for that I am profoundly grateful.

To Mary Jean Thornton, who embodies the best of the best of the best leader. It's an honor to have worked with you.

To Kathy McAfee, my coauthor and coconspirator. Your intelligence, humor, strength, beauty, and tenacity are a thing to behold. Thank you for being my Sherpa and not giving up on writing this book.

To Hannah, my daughter. We should all take a page from your play book—to find our passion and go after it. You show everyone that a straight line to a goal is never the way to get there. Keep taking the road less traveled.

To Olivia, my daughter. Your ability to spot bullshit and call it out appropriately is a true gift. I continue to be blown away by your focus, intellect, and beauty. I'm a better mom because of you and everyone you love is better for knowing you.

To Elena, my daughter. Your talent and intellect are immense. I'm more proud of HOW you accomplish things than the accomplishment itself. Keep laughing, keep your heart open, keep the faith. If God had a refrigerator, your picture would be on it.

Finally, to my husband Bruce. Look up the definition for Mensch; your name and photo would be there. You are both cool under pressure and just plain cool—the best role model to our daughters and the most magnificent husband. I don't know how I got so lucky. I won the marital lottery, for sure.

Kathy McAfee

To my husband Byron Schoenholzer who not only sees the value of publishing books, but he holds me accountable to it. A book a year? He knows that I can achieve this goal, and he gives me the time and space, encouragement (and the wine) to make it happen.

To my parents, Roz and Chuck McAfee. Thank you for giving me life, love, and a first-class education.

To my co-author Leesa Wallace. Thank you for saying "YES" to this book project. It has been an absolute joy and delight to work with you on it. Your energy, creativity, humor and sheer brilliance is contagious.

To Holly Koziol, our virtual assistant. You are truly America's Best Virtual Marketing Assistant! You not only make us look good, but you have brought us greater joy, balance, and perspective. Thank you for being on our team!

To my amazing clients who embraced this work and took it to the next level. Special thanks to Jo Yarranton, Bill Harris, Dulcy

O'Rourke, Jacquelynn Garofano, Christine Gemelli, Ben Krynick, and many more for putting these tools and strategies into practice in your organizations.

To my strategic business partners including Adrienne Milics, Barbara Healy, Karen Hinds, Gina Ohanesian, Maureen Ross Gemme, Jill Berquist, Jackie Johnson, Allison Davis, Annie Merkle, Linda Coveney, Jean Stetz-Pulchaski, Amy Dunn, Andy Thiede, Ellen Feldman Ornato, and once again, the amazing Leesa Wallace. I have learned so much from each of you. You continue to inspire and motivate me to be a better coach, trainer, business owner, and friend.

To the many participants who have completed the Sharpening Your Point training program. I encourage you to continue to invest in your professional skill set and to lead by example. Special shout out to Isaac who trained with me in 2017 as part of his organization's leadership development program. I thank you for sharing your personal story of immigrating from Korea. Since meeting you, your triumphant mantra "I got this" has become an inspiration to me and has helped me overcome many challenges. Thanks to you and your family for having the courage to come to America and start anew.

Last but not least to our publishing team at Indie Books International including Henry DeVries, Devin DeVries, Mark LeBlanc, Joni McPherson, and Denise Montgomery. You make it possible for authors and business leaders to share their thought-leadership through published books. We *love* working with you!

Authors

About Leesa Wallace

Leesa is a master at leadership development and learning strategy. She builds better leaders and has a proven method for doing that—in retail, manufacturing, financial services, professional services, pharma, startups, and nonprofits. She does this by staying true to her core mission of comforting the disturbed and disturbing the comfortable.

She's unapologetically practical and has a focus on bringing practical, realistic, integrated approaches to help elevate individual, team, and organizational performance. She connects the dots between business goals and employee behavior by bringing an ability to work at all levels in an organization and "meet people where they are."

Over a period of thirty years, Leesa has helped bring success to organizations such as GE, Deloitte, Blum Shapiro, Harbor One Bank, Bridgeport Fittings, Odyssey Reinsurance, Louis Vuitton, TJX, Tradewind Aviation, Bristol Myers Squibb and Trinity Health of New England. In 2011, Leesa gave up "working for the man" and decided to "be the man," opening her own leadership development consulting practice. She hasn't looked back and is eternally grateful for all that she learned from the gifted leaders within these organizations.

Leesa is a graduate of the University of Wisconsin-Eau Claire with a degree in communications and journalism. She completed her M.Ed in Adult Education with a concentration in management (she calls it an "MBA light") from Cambridge College.

Leesa and her husband, Bruce, are loving life as empty nesters in Bloomfield, Connecticut. Their three grown daughters have been replaced with Nico—the coolest rescue cat imaginable. She takes immense pride in knowing that "the kids are all right" and are each pursuing their dreams in their own unique ways.

Learn more about Leesa at her website:
    http://www.performance-architect.com

Connect with Leesa on LinkedIn:
    https://www.linkedin.com/in/leesa-wallace-b68a0a7/

About Kathy McAfee

Kathy McAfee is an executive presentation coach and professional speaker and is known as America's Marketing Motivator. She works with organizations who want to develop a stronger and more diverse pipeline of future leaders and a workforce that is highly engaged and motivated. She also works with consultants and independent professionals who want to become outstanding in their chosen fields.

She has expertise in the areas of communication, networking, business development, and personal branding. But if you asked her what business she is really in, she would tell you the confidence-building business.

A prolific writer, Kathy is the author of *Stop Global Boring, Networking Ahead,* 3rd edition, and coauthor of *Defining You* and soon-to-be bestseller, *Sharpening Your Point*. She is also the recipient of the prestigious Best Blog of the Year, awarded by *The Women in Business and The Professions World Awards* (2014).

For more years than she will ever admit, Kathy built her career and developed her business acumen in corporate America. She's brought marketing success to organizations such as Levi Strauss & Co., Maybelline cosmetics, and Southcorp Wines of Australia. On a three-year assignment in England, Kathy led European marketing initiatives for an international vision care company. In 2005, Kathy gave flight to her entrepreneurial dreams and launched her own consulting business, a journey she recommends to anyone with a spirit of adventure and the stomach for uncertainty.

Kathy is a graduate of Stanford University in economics (go, Cardinals!). She is a member of the National Speakers Association, a past board member for the YWCA of the Hartford Region, and an active member of Rotary International, and Soroptimist International of the Americas. A resilient woman, Kathy is also an ovarian cancer survivor and holds a second-degree black belt in the martial art of Tae Kwon Do. Kathy and her husband, Byron, their rescue dog, Sofiya, and tribe of spirited cats are enjoying life in Greenville, South Carolina, USA.

Learn more about Kathy at her website:
    http://www.americasmarketingmotivator.com/

Connect with Kathy on LinkedIn:
    https://www.linkedin.com/in/kathymcafee/

Contact Information

Leesa Wallace

Leadership Development and Learning Strategy Expert

Website: Performance-Architect.com

Telephone: 1+ (860) 604-6834

E-mail: PerformanceArchitect@comcast.net

Social Media:

LinkedIn profile: linkedin.com/in/leesa-wallace-b68a0a7/

Contact Information

Kathy McAfee

Executive Presentation Coach and Professional Speaker

Website: AmericasMarketingMotivator.com

Telephone: 1+ (860) 371-8801

E-mail: Kathy@AmericasMarketingMotivator.com

Social Media:

LinkedIn profile: linkedin.com/in/kathymcafee

Subscribe to her channel: youtube.com/user/kathymcafee

Facebook: www.facebook.com/StopGlobalBoring

Twitter: @SpeakerKathyMc

Works Referenced

Hall, Randy. "Why People Don't Do What You Say." 4th Gear Consulting, March 26, 2012. http://www.4thgearconsulting.com/blog/why-people-dont-do-what-you-say/.

Learning, Vignettes. "Story-Based ELearning Idea: Learning Objectives That Truly Matter at Work." YouTube, April 16, 2019. https://www.youtube.com/watch?v=7KfzEUm8xc8.

"List: Women CEOs of the S&P 500." Catalyst. Accessed May 30, 2019. https://www.catalyst.org/research/women-ceos-of-the-sp-500.

McNamee, Brent. "The World's Most Dangerous Game To Hunt." Huntercourse.com, November 9, 2011. https://www.huntercourse.com/blog/2011/11/the-worlds-most-dangerous-game-to-hunt/.

Medina, John. *Brain Rules: 32 Principles for Surviving and Thriving at Work, Home and School*. Pear Press, 2014.

Index

FEWER WORDS
MORE IMPACT
GREATER INFLUENCE

SHARPENING YOUR POINT

Winning the Battle for Communication Efficiency

Leesa Wallace & Kathy McAfee

Scan this QR code
to receive tips, tools,
and best practices for
Sharpening Your Point.

Or go online to:
SharpeningYourPoint.com

The password is
Sharpen.

Made in the USA
Lexington, KY
28 September 2019